Y0-BBW-822

Sister Chiara Augusta Lainati O.S.C.

SAINT CLARE OF ASSISI

EDIZIONI PORZIUNCOLA

Translated from the Italian
by Sister Jane Frances, P.C.C.

© Edizioni Porziuncola
  Via Protomartiri Francescani, 2
  06081 S. Maria degli Angeli – Assisi (PG)
  www.edizioniporziuncola.it

ISBN 978-88-270-0969-7

IV edition
June 2011

Printed by
Grafiche VD
Città di Castello (Pg)

CONTENTS

6

PREFACE

Surely there is no one who has not, at least once in his life, heard of Assisi: this symbol of peace and brotherhood, this mecca of pilgrims, this center of international tourism.

Pilgrims come to Assisi in throngs. They go from one shrine to another, seeking the vestiges of the holiness of Francis and Clare in the stones which speak of the past. They discover traces of the two saints in the timeworn wood of the little choir of San Damiano and in the cold nakedness of the rocks of the Carceri. They pray where the saints themselves prayed, and then they depart. As their train glides out of Santa Maria, or the bus descends the last steep slope of Subasio, they look back in a final farewell of eyes and heart to the massive structure built by Elias, or to the olive trees which hide San Damiano. These are the pilgrims.

But there are also those who come to Assisi motivated only by curiosity, desiring to see a place which almost everyone else has seen. They leave and their eyes are filled with the beauty of a view not easily forgotten: a range of distant mountains, a short stretch of lane climbing boldly between a festival of flower-decked balconies, a warm, roseate light cast by the stones of the many monuments.

St. Clare has much to say both to the pilgrim who pauses in devout prayer before her body (which is lovingly guarded by the Poor Clares in the crypt of the basilica dedicated to her) and to the tourist who is too hurried and distracted by the rhythm of modern life to find time to bend his knee be-

fore the saint. She teaches the former a language of confident prayer, and she witnesses to the latter that he cannot find peace any place in the world unless it is borne within, and he cannot have it within until he responds fully to God's designs for him.

This brief sketch of the life of St. Clare is for those who desire a first meeting with her, and it is not narrated in scholarly language. It is an account of pure historical truth, taken from unimpeachable documents which portray St. Clare as she is, living and real for the twentieth century, a model for people today and not merely a personality relegated to a backdrop of medieval scenery. For it is precisely the prerogative of the saints, as it is of artists of immortal masterpieces, to be alive in every age and always to speak the language of the present.

Chapter One

CLARE, DAUGHTER OF FAVARONE

Assisi at the time of the saint

It was in the year 1193, in the mild air of Assisi, that Clare first opened her eyes to the world in the house on the Piazza San Rufino long owned by her family. The city at this time was still suffering from the wounds inflicted on it by Barbarossa, who had conquered it sixteen years earlier and installed his faithful Conrad of Urlingen at the Rocca Maggiore to safeguard imperial privileges and feudal laws. The city was starkly dominated from above by the battlemented walls and mighty towers of the Rocca. For the serfs, for the common people whose stage was the daily commerce of the marketplace, and for the new middle class of wage earners, it cast a gloomy shadow. For them it symbolized the observance of feudal laws and the satisfaction of obligations due to the emperor and the lords, the *Maiores*, as these noblemen were called, in contrast to the *Minores*, consisting of the common people.

Although Assisi at that time was breathing the air of a free commune, it was still forcibly subject to the emperor and to feudal ordinances imposed by him. Discontent spread among the people. In the highest stratum, the merchants, enriched through commerce at home and abroad, struck ever more independent and arrogant stances toward the impoverished nobles in their castles. In the lower strata, the common people and the serfs often expressed their discontent in open hostility to the constituted order. This was especially true where hunger, never a harbinger of peace, carved hollows in faces and empty places in the bosoms of families. Such things were frequent in these times of continuous warfare between cities. The battles often despoiled the countryside in an instant and left desolation where grain had been ripening and trees had been laden with fruit. The potential for social conflict kept the nobility ever vigilant for signs of possible revolt. With weapons close at hand, they maintained access to the roads leading to communes hostile to Assisi where nobles might find refuge.

The family of Clare

Clare was born into a family of Maiores. The house, which was in the shadow of San Rufino, belonged to the sons of her grandfather, Offreduccio, and was one of the most eminent and wealthy in the city. Favarone, her father, and Monaldus and Scipio, her uncles, were proud of their highborn origins. The clangor of weapons and news of war resounded through the house, and the ear became accustomed to distinguishing among the many noises of the day, the pawing of the horses in the Piazza San Potente or on the road which, in those days, flanked the house as it descended from the Roman theater to an ancient gate. Inside the house, the servants bustled, and the style of life was aristocratic, as became a knightly station.

Favarone, a wealthy, nobleman, chose Ortulana as his

wife. To his riches and nobility she added a dowry of charity and piety. As was usual for the lady of the manor, she gathered about her a small group of ladies, among whom the daughters of Sir Guelfuccio were pre-eminent. Their houses were so close that they needed only to cross the Piazza San Rufino to visit Ortulana. Together with them she helped the needy and all were dedicated to works of piety and to making arduous devotional pilgrimages.

They were not content merely to follow the many pilgrims who walked the Roman roads to the tombs of Saints Peter and Paul, or even to press on beyond Rome to St. Michael the Archangel at Mount Gargano. These were not small undertakings considering that travel was fatiguing and hazardous under the best of circumstances, even when the roads did not pass through marshlands infested with fevers or other adversities. One needed only to leave Assisi in the direction of the Trasimeno Lake to collide with the «griffon,» the gonfalon of the hostile city of Perugia. Even when a journey was considered safe, there was always the danger that random bands of robbers might spring out unexpectedly and ruthlessly from some hiding place. In a word, every excursion was an uncertainty for those who risked it.

Thus, it was no small thing to travel to Rome, let alone to venture as far as St. Michael of Gargano. But these pilgrimages did not suffice for the pious wife of Favarone. Her devotion impelled her to join a group of pilgrims bound for Jerusalem. It is no wonder, therefore, that in Assisi she was known as a very devout woman, and her neighbors looked upon her with great respect and admiration.

As the time for the delivery of her firstborn drew near

Ortulana was seized with fear of the approaching danger. Her refuge, as always, was prayer. She hastened to church, knelt before a crucifix and fervently beseeched God to help her in her forthcoming hour. Years later she recounted to her little daughter Clare, to whom she had happily given birth, that while she was praying on her knees before the crucifix, she distinctly heard these words: «Do not be afraid, woman, for you will give birth in safety to a light which will give light more clearly than light itself.»

Ortulana chiseled these words into her heart so that she would never forget them. Later on they came back to her whenever she looked at Clare and discovered anew the child of light promised in her moment of fear. More than twenty years later, she repeated them to Clare's companions at San Damiano. But at that time before her confinement she repeated them to herself and, trusting in the promise, she wanted the child to have a name signifying light. For this reason the firstborn of Favarone di Offreduccio was given the name Clare at the baptismal font.

Clare's childhood

The child grew up in her mother's shadow. From her earliest years her school was Ortulana's works of piety and charity, which Clare, young as she was, strove her utmost in her small way to imitate. She received her first instruction in the faith from her mother, and from her mother she also learned to pray. But, like all children, she learned even more from Ortulana's daily example.

The cries of the starving rose from the streets and hovels of the poor quarters, reaching as far as the mansion in the Piazza San Rufino. At the end of the twelfth century Assisi passed through a period of squalor and misery that long remained famous as the time of «mortal hunger.» Ortulana compassionately tried to provide help in this hour of great destitution, and Clare, on her part, learned to deprive herself of delicacies secretly and, with the help of Bona, one of Guelfuccio's daughters, sent the food to the needy.

It was also from her mother that she learned to pray and here again, the seed fell on good soil where it yielded fruit a hundredfold. The prayers she heard she soon learned to say by herself, and since she did not have a string of beads, used in those times as rosaries are in the present day, she counted out her prayers to the Lord with a pile of pebbles.

Clare thus developed under the diligent guidance of her mother. A few years after the birth of Clare, Ortulana bore another daughter, who is better known as Agnes, the name given her by St. Francis, but whose baptismal name was probably Catherine. Several years later the third and last daughter, Beatrice, was born. When Clare was four or five years old, sudden disaster broke out in the city.

Flashes of fire in Assisi

On January 8, 1198, Pope Celestine III died, and Lothar dei Conti Segni, taking the name of Innocent III, was elected to the pontificate. His first thought was to secure the Duchy of Spoleto and in April of the same year

Duke Conrad left Assisi for Narni in order to consign the Duchy to the papal legates.

The departure of the duke was the signal to insurgence. The populace, as though by an agreed upon sign, rose up together and laid siege to the Rocca, which, even though guarded by a strong nucleus of German soldiers, was violently overthrown and razed to the ground. With the destruction of this symbol of imperial domination, consuls – the magistrates of the free commune – were appointed. However, the wrath of the people had not sufficiently vented itself in the stone-upon-stone destruction of the emperor's fortress. With the same fury, it turned against the feudal lords who, at the first outburst of war, had abandoned their mansions in the city and barricaded themselves in their castles scattered throughout the countryside.

The first castle to fall was Sassorosso, belonging to Gerardo, Leonardo and Fortebraccio, the sons of Gislerio d'Alberico; then, one by one, those belonging to the sons of Giovanni Matteo on the Montemoro hill, and Poggio San Damiano and lastly, the San Savino tower, where a strong nucleus of nobles was gathered. However, the war did not cease with the crashing of the castle towers under the weapons and fires of the commune army. The conflict moved inside the city, where the fury of the town's artisans found new targets in the nobles' palaces, most of which were clustered around the Murorotto district and the market square.

Between flashes of fire and the clamour of war the twelfth century came to an end, and the new century began with the nobility leaving Assisi and going to Perugia, the city most hated by the Assisians. Among the first to leave were the sons of Gislerio, including Leonardo, whose daughter Filippa, an infant at the time, was one of the Assisian children closest to Clare, and who was to be among the first companions to follow her in the life of poverty at San Damiano. Later on other knights, whose castles and city homes had been damaged by the people of Assisi, entered the service of Perugia. Among them was Monaldus, Clare's uncle and head of the illustrious family.

Assisi versus Perugia

The intimation by the Perugians to the Assisians that restitution of the exiles' possessions would be made was a pretext, because the undying hatred between the two rival cities broke out in a new war around the year 1200. It dragged on until 1205, then, after a brief truce, continued until 1209. Apparently headed by Monaldus, either because he was the eldest or because of his violent temper, Clare's family too participated in the Perugian war, siding, like most of the feudal lords, with the Perugians against his native city. Favarone too, like most of the feudatories, was forced to move his family to Perugia for a time, probably between the years 1202 and 1205. However brief the sojourn in Perugia, it sufficed for ten-year-old Clare to attract the affection of all who came to know her.

It is here that Clare met Filippa again. Here too, in the house in which her family had settled, she became acquainted with another child named Benvenuta. In later years she too would be among the first to follow the footsteps of Clare in the habit of penance. In the Process of Canonization, Sr. Benvenuta testified that Clare was singularly gracious and affable to all, humble of heart, upright in her actions, inspiring in all who saw her a vivid sense of the presence of God dwelling in her. This is how Clare was remembered by these two young people during her stay in Perugia, and this is the way she was remembered by relatives, acquaintances and servants who were close to her after her family returned to Assisi.

Clare's vocation

It is always difficult, if not impossible, to determine the moment in which God invites a soul to Himself, the moment we usually identify as the call of vocation. It is difficult because the moment in which the Lord makes Himself present in a soul, calling her in a very precise and personal way, rather than in a general way that could avail for anyone, remains, for the most part, a secret confined to the soul itself. It is also difficult because, more often than not, the call does not come suddenly, but gradually by a continuous, slow working of grace which permeates the soul until she distinctly recognizes the voice of Him Who calls her. But in every case, whether or not the soul is conscious of it, the birth of a vocation always necessitates a change of life. The vocation always produces a conversion (and this is precisely the term which St. Clare used to indicate the moment in which she left the world to follow Christ). Such a change of life is not always manifest exteriorly, above all in a case like that of St. Clare, in which the person called has never been far from God. Once the invitation of the Lord is perceived, even if the external life remains unchanged, the whole interior significance of her actions changes. All that she does has the sole purpose of conforming the will to God.

To determine the moment of Clare's vocation is impossible. But, observing her comportment in the house of Favarone in Assisi, we can say that God made Himself present in her soul in a precise and personal way very early in her life. By «a precise and personal way» is meant that Clare understood that she was called by God to a life spent for Him in penitence and prayer. How this was to be actuated she herself did not know until she had been enlightened by her conversations with St. Francis.

When she returned from Perugia, her behaviour seemed to be the same as it always had been. She distributed all the alms that she could, as she had learned from her mother. With the help of Bona, she secretly continued to deprive herself of food in order to give it to the poor, but this could not escape the attentive eyes of the servants for long. She prayed much, as her mother had taught her and as she had done from earliest childhood.

Love of suffering and...

There was something else apparent in her, and it is this very «something» which enables one to say unequivocally that Christ had called her and invited her to follow Him along a well-defined path: Clare loved, desired and sought suffering for the love of Christ.

St. Francis prayed on Mount La Verna, «My Lord Jesus Christ, I beg you to grant me two graces before I die: the first, that I may experience in my body and soul as much as possible that pain which you, sweet Jesus, sustained in the hour of your most bitter passion; and the second, that I might feel in my heart as much as possible that excessive love with which you, Son of God, were inflamed so that you willed to suffer so great a passion for us sinners.» Such a prayer sounds absurd to those accustomed to asking God for everything but suffering.

But Francis loved Christ and begged that he might love Him yet more with that love which opened His side and nailed His members, flesh and blood members like our own, to two crossed wooden beams. St. Bernardine of Siena said, «He who loves is always transformed into the beloved,» and so he who loves Christ cannot but love the suffering of Christ and ardently desire it with every fibre of his being and implore that it be the means of union with Him.

The measure of one's love of Christ is the measure of one's love of suffering, because it is true that «the Christian life is a continuation and a fulfillment of the life of Christ; our actions are a continuation of His actions; each one of us is another Christ who continues in his life the passion of Jesus Christ for the same intention that He had: the glory of the Father.» (A. Gemelli)

Therefore, suffering for the love of Christ and in imitation of Him gives glory to the Father. Clare, among the most noble, wealthy and beautiful («She was most beautiful,» Ranieri di Bernardo, one of her relatives said in 1253, remembering the young girl in her father's house), could no longer content herself with those sufferings which life can provide day by day. She thirsted for more, and for the glory of the Father she wore a cilice beneath her clothing, and for His glory she restricted the nourishment of her body to an irreducible minimum. More and more she sought refuge in prayer which sustained her life of penance.

...Of solitude

All about her, life continued its normal course, but, like all lovers, she was absorbed by one dominant thought. Little by little, the surrounding realities faded, leaving room only for that which Clare sensed to be coming to birth within her. Later on when her vocation became more clearly defined and she fully assented at every moment to the call of God, reality returned, more vivid through having been filtered through that pure crystal which is God. But beforehand she was occupied by one thought and nothing distracted her from it, not the crowds gathered in the Piazza San Rufino to deliberate questions important to the city, nor the throngs of cavaliers who passed in review before the cathedral. The Piazza was the meeting place of citizens, armed forces and magistrates, but no one ever saw Clare at the window of her home, because Clare, wishing neither to see nor to be seen, sought the solitude and quiet of the more secluded rooms.

Clare did not withdraw from people because of melancholia, which often afflicts those passing from adolescence to young adulthood. It was the need of solitude which accompanied His initiative, as in any vocation; it was the necessity for a deep silence in which the voice of God rising in the soul could be heard more distinctly, understood in its truest sense and enjoyed in its sweetness. Clare herself demonstrated that this was so. When the family was united and engaged in conversation, Clare participated animatedly, but on one subject only, as though she knew how to speak of one thing only: of God and the things of God. She thought of nothing else.

Her neighbors, like Bona and Pacifica di Guelfuccio,

and those who visited Favarone's home, like the eminent Ugolino di Pietro Girardone or Ranieri di Bernardo, could not but marvel at Clare's sweetness, her manner of smiling and speaking, and her conversation always centered on God. Through them the fame of her goodness emerged beyond the walls of the house and spread through the byways of Assisi.

However, the first-born of Favarone was already well known in the city. All the poor knew her through the assistance which came to them through the hands of Bona. She was known for her modesty (that is always a sign of inner purity) by would-be suitors aspiring for her hand, as they vainly raised their eyes to the windows of her house in the Piazza San Rufino. Clare did not seem to be thinking of marriage.

Refusal of marriage

It was Favarone who first talked to her about marriage. He knew it was not only good, but very good that his daughter was pious (to the point of sending Bona di Guelfuccio on a pilgrimage to St. James at Compostella), that she was charitable, that she was modest. But as Clare approached the age of seventeen, her father became concerned by her behavior, by her doing all to please God, but nothing to please men, her constant conversation about God, with no thought of anyone else.

She was noble, wealthy, beautiful and good. She had all that was requisite to a bride of one of the powerful lords of the city, and Favarone began negotiations toward this end. Clare not only refused to marry, but decidedly did not even want to hear marriage discussed. She told her father and mother that she wanted to preserve her virginity for the Lord. Urged again and again to withdraw from her resolve, she remained obstinate in her refusal. Those who, like Ranieri di Bernardo, attempted to make peace in the family by trying to convince the young lady to obey her parents, got an answer beyond the usual stubborn «no.» They heard a discourse in which Clare used all the weapons of her eloquence in begging to follow Christ in the renunciation of the pleasures of the flesh.

In the year 1210, for more than three years, all Assisi had been talking of the son of the famous merchant Pietro Bernardone, Francis who, impressively armed, left for Apulia to win knighthood. He returned home a few days after his departure and began behaving in a manner considered insane by most and holy by very few.

Chapter Two

CLARE, GIVEN TO GOD

The Son of Pietro Bernardone

The life of St. Francis of Assisi is so well known that we need devote but a rapid outline of it here. We are interested primarily in seeing what influence the sensational conversion of the son of Pietro di Bernardone, who stripped himself of everything so that he might call himself in fullest truth son of God, may have had on Clare.

The spiritual crisis which changed Francis from the Assisian «flower of youth» to the bridegroom of most perfect poverty occurred around the years 1206 to 1209, at which time Clare would have been between thirteen and sixteen years of age. This crisis gradually settled into a number of salient incidents which were like milestones in the conversion of the young man, and which were so dramatic that Clare, like all of Assisi, must surely have known of them.

The son of Pietro Bernardone was well known in Assisi. It was Francis himself, moreover, who tried in every way to be in the forefront and to draw attention to himself. This was one of the traits which marked him, in a sense, from the baptismal font. That curious name, Francis, was given to him by his father on his return from a business sojourn in France, instead of the name John, which his mother had given the baby. Among the youth of the city, Francis was outstanding for his natural gifts of cleverness and animation inherited from his merchant father, and for the magnanimity and adventuresome aspirations for knighthood inherited from his mother, Pica.

At first he was fascinated by worldly pomp. Among the common folk in the marketplace there was considerable gossip about the probable cost to Pietro of this son who, for the sake of ostentation, had a garment fashioned, half of which was made of expensive fabric and half of sackcloth. In order to be pre-eminent, he frequently had himself elected «leader of the banquet,» which meant paying all the expenses of the merrymaking for the whole party.

Then, suddenly, Francis became sated with this life and took a fancy to weaponry. One day he was seen, smartly armed down to the finest detail, departing through the St. George gate toward the road to Rome. He was headed for Apulia whence, he said, he would return as an invested knight. It seemed assured that he would come back a great prince. Instead, a few days later, with slack reins and remote expression on his face, he returned to Assisi, having suddenly lost all enthusiasm for the war venture.

Conversion of St. Francis

From that day on no one made much of his eccentricities. Francis began to search for solitary places where the noise of daily living would not intrude. He preferred the countryside where he sometimes passed entire days. In his solitary amblings through the fields, he would visit the little churches which at that time dotted the environs of the city in great numbers. One day the rumor spread through Assisi that Francis had not returned home, but was staying in a cave near the church of San Damiano. Next he was seen at the crossroads of the church of San Giorgio with tattered clothing and looking like a madman. People derided and abused him as though he were crazy, and all of Assisi was present when he stripped himself before Bishop Guido in order to return even his clothing to Pietro Bernardone. All this reached Clare's ears, and in her heart she often returned to Francis' answer to the bishop, who summoned him to return the money he had taken from his father: «My Lord, I want to return not only his money, but all of his clothing too.»

It is the way of absolute poverty which makes the following of Christ swift and sure. He who is poor, absolutely poor, to the point of not possessing even a coarse garment (as Francis possessed none, although he used one until someone asked for it in the name of the love of Christ or until someone seemed to be more in need of it than he) has no preoccupations in the material realm to impede his service of God, has nothing to defend because he possesses nothing. He lives only to serve God, entrusting himself to Him who said: «So do not worry; do not say, "What are we to eat? What are we to drink? What are we to wear?" It is the gentiles who set their hearts on all these things. Your heavenly Father knows you need them all. Set your hearts on his kingdom first, and on God's saving justice, and all these other things will be given you as well,» (*Mt* 6:31-33). It is also written, «Provide yourselves with no gold or silver, not even with coppers for your purses, with no haversack for the journey or spare tunic or footwear or a staff, for the labourer deserves his keep,» (*Mt* 10:10). Francis, guided by these

Gospel words, removed his shoes, put aside his walking stick, exchanged his belt for a cord. Thus clad in what became the habit of the Friars Minor, Francis arose to preach in Assisi.

St. Francis Preaches in Assisi

In the spring of 1209 the city was exhausted by war, and the word of St. Francis was «like a burning fire, penetrating the inmost reaches of the heart,» (*1 Celano* 23). He preached in the churches, and his greeting, «May the Lord give you peace!» resounded through the vaults like a breath of life reaching out to restive souls. He also preached in the cathedral of San Rufino. The content of his sermons was very simple. He clung to the basic truths: the four last things and the Gospel. He expounded the word of God with the ardor of one inspired. His discourses were overpowering and at the same time so plain and clear that they captured souls.

He spoke of poverty, which is to possess nothing in order to acquire everything again in God. Nor was his mere theory. All of his listeners knew that Francis was the son of the richest merchant in Assisi and that he despoiled himself of everything in order to follow the Gospel to the letter. Clare knew too, and she asked herself if God did not want the same of her, a total gift like that of Francis, abandoning everything without reserve.

It was well known to the daughter of Favarone how Francis lived with the little band of twelve gathered about him. They went from house to house begging a morsel of bread after having worked an entire day without asking recompense. Recompense was the glory of

God. Their prayer was the praise of God, the only form of prayer which does not return to self, but which rises to infinity and is content simply to be expressed. This praise of God has a thousand voices, because all of creation proclaims it. It is in the song of the skylark outlined against the sun, in the chirp of the locust in the heat of the day; yet, again, it has no voice, for the highest form of praise is in the silent adherence of the will to the most high God.

Clare felt great sympathy for this little group which asked for nothing except for the love of God, and Bona di Guelfuccio found that a new mission of charity was opening out before her. She began descending from Assisi to the little church of St. Mary of the Porziuncula where the brothers were working, bringing them money so that once in a while they could nourish themselves with something more substantial than their usual crusts of bread. In the house of the sons of Offreduccio there were also many occasions to speak of Francis. It was the year 1210, and Rufino, Clare's cousin, the son of Scipio, also chose the coarse monk's robe of Francis in preference to the comforts of the paternal home.

Clare Is Drawn in the Way of Poverty

It was poverty, the «naked following of the naked cross» of which St. Jerome spoke, which attracted others to follow in the footsteps of Francis. When it became clear to the daughter of Favarone that the total gift to Christ could be actuated only by a renunciation of every good thing, her path was forever decided. The way of Francis would also be the way of Clare. On the other hand, a program of absolute poverty for the love of Christ was not easy for a girl of noble and wealthy family to implement, particularly for a girl so young. She was not yet eighteen. If the call to total self-giving was certain for Clare, the form that this donation should take was far less evident.

The desire to renounce everything, the world and oneself, is per se an absolute. The soul which feels called by God to a total donation is stamped with an indelible imprint, a longing for the vows of chastity (the sacrifice of legitimate pleasures), of poverty (the surrender of even necessities), and of obedience (the stripping of one's own will). It was thus that Clare gave herself totally and unreservedly to Christ crucified and wished that she had more in order to render more to the Creator of all. But the manner in which this gift was to be realized she did not know. The total self-giving to God in poverty as St. Francis preached intimated an absolute abandonment to divine providence. Clare desired this abandonment, but was not clear just how it was to be brought about practically. Therefore it was necessary that Francis clarify for her the way which would bring about the will of God, the same path on which God had placed him and which would unfold as a complement to his own.

A Colloquy with Francis

And so Clare, accompanied by the faithful Bona di Guelfuccio, and unknown to her parents, called on St. Francis, who was already acquainted with her virtue, which was well known to all Assisi. In fact, the ancient biographer of St. Clare recounts that Francis, knowing by reputation of Clare's goodness, greatly desired to detach her from the world in order to give her as a total offering to God. Clare spoke with him; Bona beside her was but a shadow. Francis, who was accompanied by Friar Phillip the Long, listened. The young girl confided to him God's call and asked his help in putting it into action according to the divine plan.

«The Father Francis encouraged her to despise the world, showing her by his living speech how dry the hope of the world was and how deceptive its beauty. He whispered in her ears of a sweet espousal with Christ, persuading her to preserve the pearl of her virginal purity for that blessed Spouse Whom Love made man.» (*Legend of St. Clare*)

During St. Clare's process of canonization, Bona was asked what St. Francis used to speak about. She replied that «he always preached that the Lady Clare should be converted to Jesus Christ,» that is, that she should direct her whole life, all the movements of her soul and body to the love of Christ.

We can conjecture from many passages of his writings the sort of eloquence St. Francis would have used when speaking about God and of charity, for example this excerpt from the First Rule for the Friars Minor:

«We should wish for nothing else and have no other desire; we should find no pleasure or delight in anything except in our Creator, Redeemer, and Saviour; he alone is true God, who is perfect good, all good, every good, the true and supreme good, and he alone is good, loving and gentle, kind and understanding; he alone is holy, just, true, and right; he alone is kind, innocent, pure, and from him, through him, and in him is all pardon, all grace, and all glory for the penitent, the just, and the blessed who rejoice in heaven. Nothing, then, must keep us back, nothing separate us from him, nothing come between us and him. At all times and seasons, in every country and place, every day and all day, we must have a true and humble faith, and keep him in our hearts, where we must love, honour, adore, serve, praise and bless, glorify and acclaim, magnify and thank, the most high supreme and eternal God, Three and One, Father, Son, and Holy Spirit, Creator of all, Saviour of those who believe in him, who hope in him, and who love him; without beginning and without end, he is unchangeable, invisibile, indescribable and ineffable, incomprehensible, unfathomable, blessed and worthy of all praise, glorious, exalted, sublime, most high, kind, lovable, delightful and utterly desirable beyond all else, for ever and ever.» (Chapter 23)

And again in the paper given to Brother Leo:

«You are holy, Lord, the only God, and your deeds are wonderful. You are strong. You are great. You are the Most High, You are almighty. You, holy Father, are King of heaven and earth. You are Three and One, Lord God, all good. You are Good, all Good, supreme Good, Lord God, living and true. You are love, you are wisdom. You are humility, You are endurance. You are rest, You are peace. You are joy and gladness. You are justice and moderation. You are all our riches, and You suffice for us. You are beauty. You are gentleness. You are our protector, You are our guardian and defender. You are courage. You are our haven and our hope. You are our faith, our great consolation. You are our eternal life, great and wonderful Lord, God almighty, merciful Saviour.»

This was not merely a list of expressions. It was the fullness of a heart which, in speaking of God, was unable to articulate itself except by heaping the most exalted human qualities one upon another without, however, being able to voice that which can only find expression in adoring silence. This was how St. Francis spoke of God to Clare. And «immediately an insight into the eternal joys was opened to her at whose vision the world itself would become worthless, with whose desire she would begin to melt, [and] for whose love she would begin to yearn for heavenly nuptials.» (*Legend of St. Clare*)

It was the intuition of God, «the true, greatest good, the only good,» which Clare experienced through Francis' words, that intuition which the grace of God grants to those who seek him with a humble and sincere heart. And, as the eyes are dazzled by brilliant light such as the sun when one comes from a place of semi-darkness and are unable to distinguish objects which shortly before seemed clear, where there is complete obscurity when a few moments earlier everything could be easily discerned, so this sudden intuition of God robbed Clare of all capacity to see anything else, and everything, by comparison, seemed dark, pale and faded to her.

St. Francis as Clare's Guide

Her first conversation with the man of God was followed by others. Clare entrusted her soul to Francis so that he would guide her according to the Lord's plan, and she obeyed him in all things. «We should wish for nothing else and have no other desire; we should find no pleasure or delight in anything except in our Creator, Redeemer, and Saviour; he alone is true God, who is perfect good, all good, every good, the true and supreme good...,» Francis had told her. She no longer heard anything else. For her the sparrows which filled the quiet air of the first autumnal evenings had no other song, and when the winter snow swirled, the force of the wind which skidded along the rugged slope of Mt. Subasio and tossed the beeches and ancient oaks, spoke of nothing else. But the spring of 1211 was nearing. March advanced in the solemn rhythm of Lent. Palm Sunday, March 28, was close.

At one time, in the first centuries of Christianity, Palm Sunday was the day on which the truths of the faith and Christian morality were officially expounded to the catechumens who were to be baptized the following Holy Saturday. It was specifically Palm Sunday that Francis chose for Clare's gift of herself to God, and he also taught the girl that «renounce yourself» of which Christ speaks (*Mt* 16:24). Clare was to prove that only by self-renunciation can one obtain the promise of Christ, that «joy no one shall take from you,» (*Jn* 16:22).

The Last Day

During Clare's last visit to St. Francis he gave her the final instructions for her departure from the house. As was her custom on Palm Sunday, she was to join all the other young girls in the church of San Rufino for the ceremony of the distribution of the olive branches, and once more she was to dress herself with particular care from the array of her magnificent gowns. But the following night, the night between Palm Sunday and Monday of Holy Week, she was secretly to leave the house, appropriately accompanied, and go to St. Mary of the Porziuncula where Francis and his brothers would be waiting to consecrate her to God.

Palm Sunday: the last festive note before the tears of Holy Week. Jesus went up to Jerusalem riding a little ass, surrounded by a jubilant populace honoring him, waving palm branches and acclaiming him «King of Israel.» But Jesus was thinking of the approaching hour, the hour of the Passion and said, «My soul is troubled. And what shall I say? Father, save me from this hour? But it is for this very reason that I have come to this hour. Father, glorify your name,» (*Jn* 12:27-28). Across the centuries Palm Sunday has retained this intrinsic characteristic of a joyous exterior coinciding with a sorrowing interior, intimating the approaching hour. From this arises a sense of sadness, a painful disquiet which is dispelled only by a total abandonment to the will of God.

The atmosphere in the cathedral of San Rufino was festive with a soft springtime light pouring into the nave through the rose window and with the display of gala multi-colored gowns and the rustle of olive branches which Bishop Guido was distributing to all. The group of young noblewomen were a harmony of color and rejoicing. At last it was their turn to approach the altar to take some palm: one, another, and then another. Then it was Clare's turn. But Clare did not move. All eyes were fixed on her. Why did she not go? Was she absorbed in prayer, or distracted, or did she not dare to venture between the two aisles of people whose eyes were fixed on her? All were waiting in suspense. But only for a moment. As though it were the most natural thing in the world, Bishop Guido descended the altar steps, approached Clare and handed her the palm. Had Clare, perhaps, just finished saying to herself, «I have come precisely for this hour. Father, glorify your name»?

The Flight from the Paternal Home

Evening fell, a normal evening at the end of a festive day. No one in the house knew anything. None of Clare's friends and companions were aware of her plan. Bona, the only one who had followed Clare's vocation step by step from its birth to its resolution in her total assent to the Lord, was not in Assisi at the moment of its consummation. She was in Rome for Lent. The darkness became pitch black as little by little evening yielded to night. The hour had come. The silence kept repeating to Clare, «No one who prefers father or mother to me is worthy of me,» (*Mt* 10:37).

The young girl directed her steps to one of the secondary doors of the house. It would have been too risky to leave through the main door which opened onto the square. Here, however, she seemed to face the first serious obstacle: the door was barred with heavy beams and with a stone pillar that would have discouraged anyone's daring. But Clare had to go. She was strengthened by the thought that it was now or never, and that the door would open toward the supreme liberty of which Francis had enamoured her, that liberty which is to serve God, moment by moment, in absolute fidelity to his word. And the door opened. It was thrown wide to the obscurity of full nightime. «The Lord is my shepherd... By tranquil streams He leads me. He guides me in paths of saving justice. Even were I to walk in a ravine as dark as death I should fear no danger, for you are at my side. Your staff and your crook are there to soothe me,» (*Ps* 23:1-4).

CHAPTER THREE

SAN DAMIANO

Clare at the Porziuncula

Down in the valley in the dense woods the brothers were keeping a prayer vigil at the little church of St. Mary of the Porziuncula as they awaited the arrival of Clare. When they heard the young woman and her companion approaching, they went out with lighted torches to meet them. Clare entered the church and prostrated before the altar of the Virgin Mary. She sealed her consecration with the cutting of her flowing tresses. With this act, Clare intended to strip herself of every external thing and to dedicate herself wholly to the Lord. With this gesture, which henceforth separated her from the world, while giving her a possession of it that was more real and more fulfilling, she was made the «sister, spouse and mother of the Son of the Most High Father and of the glorious Virgin,» (*Letter* I). She was clothed as a fresh «springtime» (*Letter* I) with that new and unique joy which the Lord alone knows how to give when he wholly possesses his creature. It took but a moment to say «yes» kneeling before the Virgin of the angels, but it was a «yes» that endured for the whole of her life.

Francis then hastily led Clare to the protection of a Benedictine monastery, that of St. Paul of the Abbesses, located near the site of the present Bastia, which is not far from Assisi. It is certain that Clare, in doing this, had no intention of embracing the Benedictine Rule; otherwise it would have made no sense for her to flee during the night to the Porziuncula and, in naked faith beyond every human structuring, abandon herself to the heavenly Father through the hands of Francis. A future daughter of St. Benedict would have taken shelter immediately in a Benedictine monastery where she would have been consecrated and, in the normal ways, would have bound herself definitively to their Rule.

But Clare was not a daughter of St. Benedict and St. Scholastica. She was not at this time making vows to adhere to any particular Rule, but giving herself to God without restrictions of any kind. She looked at the cross and, without turning back followed it in the poverty which alone could make it light, in the chastity which alone permitted her to turn her eyes entirely to God, in the obedience which divested her of self just as poverty uncluttered her of things. In pronouncing her «yes» she felt no need of a Rule; anything else would have seemed to her a restriction of the totality of her gift.

Reaction to Clare's Flight

Accompanying Clare to the Benedictine monastery was only a prudent act on the part of St. Francis, who envisioned the tempest which would quickly erupt among her relatives and which did, indeed, explode as soon as Favarone's household became aware of the escape of the firstborn. They marveled that, unaided, she had been able to release the heavy bars which obstructed the door.

They discovered where she had taken refuge and rushed to St. Paul of the Abbesses with the intention of bringing the fugitive back to her home. But, like all convents and churches and sacred places, the monastery of St. Paul enjoyed the right of asylum, and excommunication was imposed on anyone committing violence of any sort to those who have taken refuge there. Therefore, Clare did not have to fear that she might be torn away by main force. But there are other forms of violence not subject to excommunication which can inflict far more on the soul than can great physical force on the body. It was to this kind of violence that the family resorted. For days they persisted in asking her to return, first reminding her of the pleasure of intimate hours spent at home with her mother and sisters, then flashing before her eyes a future of terrestrial happiness, later accusing her of ingratitude, and finally having recourse to insults and threats.

But Clare did not yield. In the end, after several days of torment, she resorted to an action which had the power to terminate further insistence on the part of the relatives. Holding herself erect by the altar cloth, as though to draw strength from it, and, at the same time finding it a shield of defense, she tore off her veil and headband, disclosing her shorn head, the sign of her belonging to Christ alone. Clare was no longer a beautiful young lady of this world. Clare was no longer the first-born daughter of a wealthy, noble Assisian. Clare no longer gave a thought to human happiness. She placed all her hope in Christ alone. She seemed to say all this in her gesture, and in the face of her sheer intrepidity, the confused family could do nothing but submit and depart.

St. Francis, Brother Philip and Brother Bernard accompanied her from St. Paul's because Clare's residence

in a Benedictine monastery, although justified in anticipation of the family's attack, could not be unduly prolonged since Clare had no intention of embracing the
Rule of St. Benedict. Or, perhaps it was the nuns themselves who encouraged her departure, given the uproar
her presence in the monastery provoked. Nevertheless,
another Benedictine monastery opened its arms to the
young girl, the monastery of Sant'Angelo di Panzo, on
the eastern slope of Mt. Subasio, along the upper road to
Spello, outside the Porta Antica. The monastery has disappeared now. According to an evocative legend it was
named for the angel of reconciliation: *Angelus pacis*.

Her Sister Agnes

Sixteen days had elapsed since Clare left her home
when she was joined at Sant'Angelo by her young sister,
whom tradition knows by the name of the invincible Roman virgin Agnes. She said that she had come to serve
the Lord completely, and Clare, who loved her sister so
deeply, had prayed incessantly that God would call her to
follow the same path. She could do nothing but exult,
praise and thank the Lord when he made sisters in
shared ideals these two who were sisters in the flesh. The
joyous embrace of the two sisters made Agnes the first
follower of Clare in the poverty of Christ.

Agnes' Resistance

This time, however, Favarone decided that he was going to have his daughter back, dead or alive. Monaldus

placed himself at the head of a band of twelve men who set off at a gallop for Sant'Angelo di Panzo.

«They were filled with rage, yet they concealed their cunning purpose under a calm and peaceful exterior and then entered the place. Turning to Agnes, for they had now given up all hope concerning Clare, they said: "Why did you come to this place? Get ready at once to return home with us." When she answered that she was resolved never to leave Clare, one of the knights, unable to contain his fury any longer, rushed upon her and brutally assailed her with blows and kicks, and then seizing her by the hair, began to drag her away. The others had, meanwhile, run forward to assist their companion, lifting her up in their arms to carry her away. Agnes, finding herself seized, as it were by savage beasts, and snatched away from the embrace of her Divine Lord, loudly called upon Clare, saying: "Help me, my dearest sister, and do not permit me to be separated from my Lord!" Her captors were still dragging her down the slope of the hill, Agnes resisting with all her might. Her garments had been torn to pieces and her hair was scattered about in handfuls. Clare had meanwhile fallen on her knees, beseeching her Divine Lord with tears in her eyes, to endow her sister's soul with fortitude and bring to naught the attempts of men by His Almighty Power.

«Suddenly the body of Agnes became so firmly rooted to the ground and so heavy, that all of them with their united efforts could not carry her over a little brook they had to cross. They asked a number of men who were engaged in the vineyards and in the fields close by to help them. But even then they could not raise the body in the least. Seeing themselves baffled in their attempt, some of them treated the evident miracle in a scoffing fashion, saying: "She must have been eating lead all night; no wonder she is so heavy." But when one of her uncles, Count Monaldus, in his rage drew his poignard to stab her, the hand which held the weapon was seized with a most acute pain which troubled him for a good while after. At this juncture, Clare appeared upon the scene of conflict and begged her kinfolk to desist from all further attempts and to leave Agnes, who lay half dead, to her care.» (Translated from *The Legend of St. Clare,* by Marianus Fiege, O.F.M. Cap.)

Monaldus and his friends returned to Favarone without the girl, who had suddenly become too heavy for the arms of a band of vigorous men. But the relating of the foregoing episode is incomplete without adding that what Monaldus' friends could not do, Clare could. While Agnes, half-dead from the blows, lay there amidst the olive trees near the brook, which Monaldus' ruffians were unable to cross with the weight of Agnes in their arms, Agnes joyfully jumped up and returned to Sant'Angelo with Clare. Shortly thereafter, St. Francis also clothed her in the habit and consecrated her to the Lord for ever.

Clare at San Damiano

Sant'Angelo di Panzo was not the place chosen by the Lord for Clare. Guided by St. Francis, she went to God by a spiritual path different from that of the Benedictines. After a few days there St. Francis conducted her to a little monastery adjacent to a small church outside the walls of Assisi. Today everyone looks upon the church and monastery of San Damiano as the sanctuary of poverty.

San Damiano is a place of pilgrimage. It attracts

people and then remains in the hearts of most of them, because of the feeling of poetry which hovers over the little cloister, or the cypresses that project above the enclosure wall, making an impression all their own, or the characteristic timbre of the little bell. But San Damiano is not simply poetry. True Franciscanism is reduced to poetic sentimentalism only by those who look at it from the outside without making an effort to penetrate it; by those who invent a St. Francis who is all sweetness as he leans down to admonish the wolf, the image so often reproduced in majolica, but who do not know the St. Francis who, wounded and bleeding, came down from La Verna conformed to Christ. For those who know how to find reality beneath the commonplace, San Damiano is the symbol of true Franciscanism. But perhaps to discover it, one must go there in the spiritual state of the young Francis.

Wandering through the fields during the spiritual torment which preceded his conversion, he found himself near the small dilapidated church. He entered and stood before the crucifix; his heart was roused by his yearning search for something indefinite and indefinable which would assuage the dissatisfaction of his soul. His was a search common to men of that time and to our own as well: «Lord, what would You have me do»?

From the regal Byzantine cross the voice of Christ spoke to Francis. San Damiano speaks to us in the simple nakedness of the walls, the rough planks which are not even squared off – poor materials gathered from here and there – of the so-called «little choir,» the steep, dark stairs which give access to the oratory and dormitory of St. Clare and her companions. There is nothing in San Damiano which does not speak of poverty and prayer, nothing which does not invite to simplicity, to search for

God alone, and which makes everything that is superfluous seem an insupportable weight.

We always depart from this oasis of peace thirsting for simplicity, desiring to carry away with us as we re-enter our world this true Franciscanism, which is to seek only the glory of God in all our actions through the constant imitation of Christ. No outward sign is needed in order to live Franciscanism. Clare remained in this poor little nest until her death. She lived forty-two years enclosed within these walls, forty-two years of prayer, silence, poverty, penitence and charity toward her sisters.

The First Companions and the First Rule

Shortly after she entered San Damiano, Clare was joined by Benvenuta of Perugia and Pacifica, who had been a frequent visitor at her home since childhood. Soon the fame of her deed spread even further and, following in her footsteps, other young women came to San Damiano desiring to belong to this evangelical group, whose only banner was the humility and poverty of Christ and whose only aim was to follow Christ to the cross, living as «Poor Sisters» in fraternal communion, fully open to the Spirit of the Lord. The Order which was coming to birth at San Damiano seemed to Clare like a «little flock whom God the Father brought forth in his holy Church by the preaching and example of the blessed Father Francis in following the poverty and humility of his own beloved Son and of his glorious Virgin Mother,» (*Testament of St. Clare*).

Besides the names of these first companions of St. Clare, there remains the testimony of their holiness of life. Drawn by the example of Clare, they learned to give without stint, to be faithful to the ideals of their Mother without stooping to any compromise. Balvina di Martino joined Benvenuta, as did Filippa, the daughter of Leonardo Gislerio the following year. Upon entering San Damiano, they all followed the example of Clare in promising obedience to St. Francis, who, on his part, was ever anxious for the little community of Damianites, and after a period during which he tested their courage, he gave them a Rule to observe.

«And observing, indeed, that we did not fear any poverty, labor, trial, scorn and contempt of the world, but rather that we held them as great delights, the blessed Father, moved by compassion, wrote for us a form of life as follows:

"Since by divine inspiration you have made yourselves daughters and hand-maids of the most high sovereign King, the heavenly Father, and have espoused yourselves to the Holy Spirit by choosing to live according to the perfection of the holy Gospel, I will and I promise for myself and my Brothers always to have for you, even as for them, loving care and special solicitude."

«This promise he lovingly fulfilled while he lived, and he wished it always to be fulfilled by his Brothers.» Thus wrote St. Clare in the Rule which synthesizes the form of life of San Damiano and which was approved by the Holy See in 1253.

The diligent care and special solicitude which Francis and his companions had for Clare and the Damianites were often preceded by the care and solicitude which divine providence had for them. Pacifica di Guelfuccio testified to a miraculous happening which occurred during the summer of 1213. There was not one drop of oil left in the monastery, not even the little that was necessary to prepare the food for the sick sisters. St. Clare summoned Friar Bentenvenga whose charge it was to beg for the monastery, and she asked him to beg for a little oil for the love of God. She washed a small vessel and placed it atop the low wall next to the gate so that the friar could take it. The empty container remained there briefly, just long enough for the brother to reach the gate, but when he picked it up, he realized at once that it was full, and he left muttering to himself about nuns who cause a man to waste time by calling him needlessly. This is how the providence of God operated directly in response to Clare's faith.

A Group Called to Live the Gospel

Going back to the very first years at San Damiano, we have the well known testimony of Jacques de Vitry-sur-Seine, who, consecrated bishop of Acre (Tolemaide, Akkon), wrote a letter from Genoa before leaving for the East in 1216: «I found one consolation in those parts (referring to his residence at the Papal Curia in Perugia), neverthless: many men and women, rich and worldly, after renouncing everything for Christ, fled the world. They are called "*Friars Minor*". They are held in great esteem by the Lord Pope and the cardinals. They do not occupy themselves with temporal affairs, but work each day with great desire and enthusiastic zeal to capture those souls that were perishing from the vanities of the world... They live according to the form of the primitive Church of which it is written: "The multitude of believers was of one heart and one soul." They go into the cities and villages during the day, so that they convert others, giving themselves to active work; but they return to their hermitages or solitary places at night, employing themselves in contemplation.

«*The women live together near the cities in various hospices* (hospitiis, small convents). *They accept nothing, but live from the work of their hands. In fact, they are very much offended and disturbed because they are honored by the clergy and laity more than they deserve.*»

To an observer outside the Order, the Poor Ladies appeared in 1216 as being of the same piece as the Friars Minor. Like the friars, they were characterized by the renunciation of the world and the abandoning of the secular. Also like the friars, they gave no thought to temporal goods, but wanted only to win souls for Christ. They renewed the experience of the primitive Church in their fraternal living in «one heart and one soul.» They accepted no possessions. They were poor in the same way as the Friars Minor. Like Francis and his companions they lived by the work of their hands.

Furthermore, there was no mingling of the Friars Minor with the Poor Ladies as in the mixed penitential confraternities flourishing at the time. On the contrary, it is clear from the testimony that the Poor Sisters did not live the same type of life as the Friars Minor. The friars were itinerants. The Poor Ladies lived in small secluded monasteries «near the cities.» The friars were scattered through the world. The Poor Ladies, however, lived a community life. («The women live together.») The friars periodically met together in chapters. The Poor Ladies never left their monasteries.

These few brush strokes suffice to distinguish the Poor Sisters from any other Order or association of the time. Clare and her sisters, the «daughters whom Francis had won for the Lord dwelt» (*1 Celano* 116), daughters of one of his inspirations from the Holy Spirit, were something entirely new in religious life witnessed in the Church up to that time. Together with the Friars Minor it was a new Order with characteristics which were revolutionary and surprising, an Order which acquired from Francis all the evangelical qualities of the movement: the following of the poor and humble Christ in fraternity within a group, while transferring the «itinerant» characteristic of the First Order to the level of faith and hope.

Guided by Francis, Clare and her sisters did not hesitate to dispossess themselves as he had done. With him, they penetrated deeply into the mystery of the poor crucified Christ. Together with Francis they embraced with absolute singleness of purpose, and with the fidelity of women with virginal hearts, the unique program of a pure following of the Gospel guided entirely by the Spirit of the Lord.

The fruit was a fraternity within the ambit of the religious family in which the members were «brothers» and «sisters;» the fraternity was universal and with all creatures; union ultimately with «the King of Glory» who inebriates the soul with joy in a nuptial experience wherein the human being loses himself in the beatitude of the sovereign Good.

The entire spiritual adventure of Francis was relived to the utmost by Clare and her sisters, not only in the highest poverty, which Clare defended strenuously to the end of her life, but also in the fruition of «the hidden sweetness that God Himself has reserved from the beginning for those who love Him,» (*Letter* III).

Thus, penetrated by the charism of Francis and in obedience to the same spirit which worked through him, the Second Order developed along the same royal way as the First Order:

> *«to do penance»*: «After the most high heavenly Father deigned by his grace to enlighten my heart that I should do penance after the example and teaching of our most blessed Father St. Francis...,» (*Rule of St. Clare* VI);
>
> *«to follow the Gospel»*: «The Form of Life of the Poor Sisters which the blessed Francis founded is this: to observe the holy Gospel of our Lord Jesus Christ...,» (*Ibid*. I);
>
> *«to live in highest poverty»*: «We shall forever observe the poverty and humility of our Lord Jesus Christ and His most holy Mother and the holy Gospel, which we have resolutely promised...,» (*Ibid*. XII);
>
> *«in Christian fraternity»*: «Let them always be solicitous to preserve intact among themselves the unity of mutual love which is the bond of perfection,» (*Ibid*. X);
>
> *«in fidelity to the Catholic Church»*: «Always submissive and subject at the feet of that holy Church, unwavering in the Catholic faith...,» (Ibid. XII).

The whole picture of the cloistered contemplative dimension places the Second Order beside the First Order as its functional complement in order to achieve a single body in the whole Christ, who preaches to the crowds without ever interrupting his colloquy in the solitude of the mountain, in the mystery of the Father.

Clare as Abbess

The relationship between St. Francis and St. Clare was, above all, that of father and daughter in a bond of faith and obedience. Three years after her entrance at

San Damiano, Clare, in obedience to St. Francis and to the bishop of Assisi, accepted the burden of abbess which she exercised to the end of her life. She never considered it an honor but an onerous service which obedience alone could have made her accept. To this end she wrote in her Rule (Chapter IV), mindful of the recommendations which St. Francis made with regard to the minister general of the Friars Minor (*2 Celano* 185):

> «The one elected should reflect upon what kind of burden she has taken up and to whom an account of the flock entrusted to her is to be rendered. She should also strive to lead the way for the others more by virtue and holy behavior than by her office so that roused by her example the Sisters might obey her more out of love than out of fear. Let her be free from exclusive friendships, lest if she love some more than others, she should cause scandal among all. Let her console the afflicted. Likewise, let her be the last refuge of the troubled...» (*Rule of St. Clare* IV).

Humility

These are not mere words. The greater the position of her who is placed at the head by obedience, the more must she consider herself inferior to all, truly «minor» like Francis. She must retain for herself the most humble tasks in the community, considering it an honor to serve the sisters at table and to wash the feet of the extern sisters when they return to the monastery. It was not a rare occurrence for the nuns to see their abbess quickly bend down and kiss the sisters' feet she was washing.

Charity

If Clare was a faithful example to her sisters in that
humility which the Poverello taught, she was no less a
loving mother to them. During the freezing nights of the
Assisian winters when the north wind made the shutters
groan and penetrated all the window frames, her hand
was always quick to cover the sleeping sisters lest they be
cold. Although rigorous with herself in the observance of
fasting and penance, Clare wanted temperance in these
for her daughters who were incapable of sustaining
greater severity, and her eye was always quick to notice
the least sign of discouragement, of distress or trial or
temptation. In these instances, she immediately summoned the sister to herself to comfort her privately with
all the words which love brought to her lips. And when
the consolation did not seem sufficient to calm the anxiety, her words yielded to tears.

Such was her overflowing love that when at times
she encountered hardness of heart in a daughter, she
threw herself at her feet and, with sweet words and ma-
ternal gestures, brought her to the path of amendment.
For Clare it was not sufficient that her daughters enjoy
God's peace. She could not bear to see them suffer physi-
cally and would lovingly raise her hand to trace the sign
of the cross on the infirmity, which would immediately
disappear.

Thus, with a simple sign of the cross she cured Sister
Benvenuta of Madonna Diambra of a purulent sore under her arm, and Sister Amata who had been immobile
for thirteen months due to dropsy and who was so
bloated from the malady that she could not even bow her
head, and Sister Andrea of Ferrara and Sister Cristiana

who had been deaf for many years, and Sister Benvenuta of Perugia who had completely lost her voice. In the course of the years between Clare's entrance into San Damiano and her death, God healed many other sisters through her hands.

The abbess of the Damianites truly strove to «lead the way for the others more by virtue and holy behavior than by her office...,» to console the afflicted, to be the refuge of the troubled. In this she became such a mirror of perfection, according to the unanimous testimony of the Poor Sisters at the process of canonization, that her daughters had in her the living example of the Rule and of fidelity to the charism of Francis.

Strength

If Clare's hand moved lightly to readjust the counterpane over a sleeping daughter, the same hand was quick to ring the bell which summoned the sisters to choir again for the midnight hour of Matins, to light the lamps in church, to awaken the sisters silently, and with special signs to rouse those who did not get up at the sound of the bell.

Mistress of the spirit, «first of all she taught them to drive every noise away from the dwelling place of the mind so that they might be able to cling to the depths of God alone.... She encouraged them to consider the demands of the flesh as insignificant and to restrain the frivolities of the flesh with reins of reason,» wrote the ancient biographer (*Legend of St. Clare* 36).

But here, too, the saint preferred to teach by her actions rather than by her words, understanding that example draws one on far more effectively than a long discourse. When mortifying the flesh and when remembering the sufferings of Christ, she subjected herself to penitence and fasts which wrung new tears from her daughters each time.

Mortification

She was happy wearing a tunic made of coarse, half-wool, homespun cloth like that used by the Umbrian peasants. Beneath the tunic she wore a biting cilice which she kept hidden from the sisters lest they remonstrate with her. Sister Benvenuta of Perugia narrated that the saint «...had a certain shirt made of boar's hide. She wore it secretly under the woolen tunic with the skin and its bristles close to her skin. Likewise, another time, she had another shirt made of horsehair, knotted with certain cords. She tied it around her body...,» (*Process of Canonization* II). One of the sisters, Sister Agnes of Oportulo, wanting to imitate her Mother in the way of penance, finally succeeded, after considerable insistence, in borrowing one of her cilices. She was able to tolerate it only three days, after which she returned it to the saint.

At night Clare lay on the ground with a stone from the river serving as her pillow. Only occasionally did she permit herself to sleep upon some vines. Later still, when her body became too weakened, Francis commanded that she lie on a pallet of straw. She also practiced extraordinary fasting.

In the third letter to Saint Agnes of Prague who had questioned her on the subject she wrote, «But our flesh is not bronze nor is our strength that of stone. No, we are frail and inclined to every bodily weakness! I beg you, therefore, dearly beloved, to refrain wisely and prudently from an indiscreet and impossible austerity in the fasting that you have undertaken. And I beg you in the Lord to praise the Lord by your very life, to offer the Lord your reasonable service and your sacrifice always seasoned with salt.»

This is the counsel of moderation which Clare gave to one of her followers. However, she was far from following her own counsels, so that it could be repeated of her that which Thomas of Celano said of St. Francis: that his fasts and penances were the only instances in which there was discordance between his words inviting discretion and his own mode of action characterized by the most severe austerity. It was the same with St. Clare who was quite right when she called herself more than once in her writings «the little plant of the holy Father Francis.»

Although she bade Agnes to be moderate, on her own part she practiced such abstinence «that seemed impossible for a person to perform,» according to the testimony of Sister Balvina di Martino (*Process of Canonization* VII). Indeed, for a long time she took no food at all on Monday, Wednesday or Friday. During the Great Lent which precedes Easter and the so-called St. Martin's Lent in preparation for Christmas, she was sustained by only bread and water except Sundays when she consented to take a little wine if they had some. Thus, days of total abstinence were followed by days of fasting on bread and water.

These mortifications which she imposed on her body would prepare a crown of real martyrdom for which she yearned. Jesus affirmed that there is no greater proof of love than to give one's life for the beloved. When Clare learned of the martyrdom of the first Friars Minor in Mo-

rocco in 1220, she would have liked to leave San Damiano to follow their example. This is the sole occasion, according to the sources, that the saint wanted to leave the
enclosure, urged only by the desire to give that witness to
God which Jesus called the greatest proof of love.

Obedience

The fasting and penances to which Clare subjected
herself (particularly the total abstention from food three
days a week) seriously affected her health. For this reason St. Francis and the bishop of Assisi intervened and
commanded, under obedience, that she eat at least 1 1/2
ounces (about 50 grams) of bread on those three days.
Clare obeyed.

It has been said elsewhere that the intimacy between
St. Francis and St. Clare was, above all, the relationship
between father and daughter in a bond of faith and obedience. We have seen St. Francis intervene in her life first
to make her accept the office of abbess, and then to
oblige her to abandon the practice of excessive austerity
in fasting. Popular legend concerning the relationship of
the two saints has been laced with many anecdotes almost always charming and endowed with a loveliness all
their own. But we are not going to relate any of them
here because, beautiful as they are, not one is as beautiful as the truth of the relationship that existed between
Francis and Clare: two human beings who gave each
other the reciprocal joy of seeing the Lord loved as each
of them wished to love him; two human beings born of
the one Spirit in order to effectuate a single program, the
limpid and unswerving following of the Gospel in a com-

plementary function. It is worthwhile deepening our understanding of the unity of the charism of Francis and Clare, of the First and Second Franciscan Orders.

St. Francis and the Poor Sisters of San Damiano

The two Orders, that of the Friars Minor and of the Poor Sisters of St. Clare, were born as one Order of the unique inspiration in the heart of St. Francis at the beginning of his conversion. From the time that Francis first experienced God (it began on a starry night along the by-paths of Assisi), the Spirit of the Lord began stripping him, and having detached him from the world, God summoned him back into the world to wander, poor and emptied of self, to recall everyone to penitence, to bring the message of peace, and to break the bread of the Word and the love of the God-Man with his fellow men.

It was in this first moment that Francis, alone before God in the solitude near San Damiano, discovered himself utterly free from everything, free to go about singing as «the herald of the Great King» along the byroads of the world, bound only to Christ «in the vastness of the open air cloister,» in a convent constructed of fresh air, of fields, of grass and of distant mountains. It was in this moment that the Spirit of the Lord summoned Clare to Francis' side as a complement to his own vocation.

Clare was a «poor madonna»* within the four walls of the same San Damiano in which Francis' vocation had become clear through the words which emanated from

---

* «Madonna» is a title of respect given to a high born lady in the Middle Ages and Renaissance times.

the crucifix: «Go, Francis, and rebuild my house....» This was both his vocation to follow Christ and his mission. Clare was a «madonna enclosed» in the secret of God in a long night of silence and contemplation to continue forever the colloquy of Francis, «most vile worm,» with the «most sweet God.»

It was not that St. Francis had planned an Order of Poor Ladies there at San Damiano, but he simply foresaw it in the same Spirit which, in a context of prayer, had become a clarification of his own vocation. The sources are clear on the subject:

«The first work that blessed Francis undertook after he had gained his freedom from the hand of his carnally minded father was to build a house of God. When he had returned to the place where the church of San Damiano had been built in ancient times, he repaired it zealously within a short time with the help of the grace of the Most High,» (*1 Celano* 18).

«Most fervently he stirred up everyone for the work of that church and speaking in a loud voice in French, he prophecied before all that there would be a monastery there of holy virgins of Christ. For always when he was filled with the ardor of the Holy Spirit, he burst forth in French,» (*2 Celano*, 13).

«While working there with other men, he called out loudly and joyfully in French to the passers-by: "Come and help us do this work for the church of San Damiano which will become a monastery of women whose life and fame will cause our heavenly Father to be universally glorified."» (*Legend of the Three Companions* VII).

«It is not to be thought that it was to repair a church that would perish and was falling down that Christ spoke to Francis from the wood of the cross.... But, as the Holy

Spirit had once foretold, the Order of holy virgins was to be established there, which, like a polished mass of living stones, was one day to be brought there unto the restoration of the heavenly house,» (*2 Celano* 204).

The goal of Francis and Clare was one: to restore the Church. And the charism was one. It was Francis who affirmed it, «saying that one and the same spirit had led the brothers and the poor ladies out of the world,» (*Ibid.* 204).

Thus, the Franciscan Second Order came into being through the working of the Spirit of the Lord during the same months in which Francis, impelled by the Spirit, decided to abandon the world and to consecrate himself totally to God. From that moment, Clare existed in the heart and mind of Francis as «the poor lady,» the «Christian woman,» as he used to call her according to Brother Stephen of Narni, which the Spirit of the Lord raised up at his side to live the same calling, the same experience of faith and the same Gospel life, not in a parallel dimension, as is sometimes erroneously affirmed, but as a complement to that which Francis himself lived.

From this perspective of complementarity it is no wonder that, under Francis' hands (he who to the end would have the wide open world as his only convent and would omit in the *Regula Bullata* even the vague allusion in the *First Rule* to the «hermitages and other places» in which, at times, the friars might find themselves), there arose a dwelling built of real and lasting stones for a monastery of Poor Ladies.

There is but one Franciscan vocation: to re-live Christ. But here below there is only one way to re-live Christ totally in his inmost being (totally for the Father and at the same time totally for men), and it is to be a unity of Francis and Clare. The single Franciscan inspiration is thus articulated in two dimensions: the contemplative, that of openness to the Word, and the active, that of witnessing to the Word. Both are dimensions of love, which is at once contemplative and active. When love labors it dreams of repose with the Beloved, and when it is resting in him it dreams of great undertakings to testify to its love.

Francis wandered through the world, free to re-live the poverty and obedience of the Son of God in the «vastness of the wide open cloister,» testifying to the Gospel in words and works. In 1216 Jacques de Vitry wrote, «They (the Friars Minor) go into the cities and villages during the day, so that they convert others, giving themselves to active work; but they return to their hermitages or solitary places at night, employing themselves in contemplation,» like the Lord Jesus.

Clare, instead, was a woman of faith and poverty at San Damiano, enclosed in an unending silence like Mary, the Mother of the Lord. She was like virgin soil, continually open wide to the Spirit of the Lord, so that Francis and his friars could completely repair the Church with their poor and humble lives as servants of the Most High. The witness of silence of this woman of the Gospel was no less efficacious than was that of Francis.

The «secret of the King» which enamored Francis in his moments of solitude next to San Damiano was always to be the secret of Clare, beyond the threshold of the mystery of God, alone on the mountain like Christ (*Mt* 14:23; *Lk* 6:12, 9:18, 9:28; *Mk* 6:31,32; *Jn* 6:15). It was a poverty which humbly, contemplatively extended to the Infinite, harboring the Spirit for the Order and for the whole Church. This was Francis' intuition, inspired by the Spirit of the Lord, as he rebuilt San Damiano. For this reason he did not hesitate from the beginning to call the Poor Ladies «Spouses of the Holy Spirit» in the little Primitive Rule, precisely the same expression he employed for the Virgin Mary in the antiphon of his *Office of the Passion of the Lord*. And in Clare Francis rediscovered himself at every moment, even in moments of darkness and doubt, for Clare's heart was wide open to the mystery of Christ, «who, laid poor in a manger, lived poor in the world, and remained stripped on the cross,» (*Testament of St. Clare*).

When, at the beginning of his religious life he did not know whether the Lord wanted him to be a preacher along the highways of the world or a solitary contemplative in a hermitage, it was Clare, together with Brother Sylvester, who, after praying, manifested the Lord's will to him. Clare was a helpmate for Francis, placed beside him by God in a complementary function, a «helper suitable for the man» (*Gen* 2:20). In Clare, whatever the situation, the whole Order continued uninterruptedly that tremendous colloquy, not of words but of the experience of love and of human poverty with «the Most High, Omnipotent and Good Lord.»

A single inspiration, therefore, blossomed in the soul of Francis. It grew as a single tree in two directions which were different but complementary. It was also a growth without the least alloy, a purity of expression before the Lord God, precisely because the two dimensions were not parallel but complementary. The functions were diverse in the body of a single origin.

In this purity of expression Francis wanted to be an example to all his friars. He did not visit the Poor Ladies of San Damiano frequently, to the point of calling forth reproof from his companions and of having to justify himself in their eyes. «Do not believe, dearest brothers, that I do not love them perfectly. For if it were a fault to cherish them in Christ, would it not have been a greater fault to have united them to Christ?... But I give you an example, that as I have done to you, so you also should do. I do not want anyone to offer himself of his own accord to visit them, but I command that unwilling and most reluctant brothers be appointed to take care of them, provided they be spiritual men, proved by a worthy and long religious life,» (2 *Celano* 205).

He kept scrupulously to his promise of spiritual assistance, «with loving care and special solicitude» (*Rule* VI), assigning to the Poor Ladies a chaplain of the Order of Friars Minor with a companion priest and two lay brothers «to support them in their poverty» (*Ibid*. XII). The relations between the two saints were indicated by some of the anecdotes recounted by St. Clare's companions. The curing of Friar Stephen is one example. It was Sister Benvenuta of Perugia who recounted it: one of Francis' brothers showed signs of derangement. St. Francis sent him to San Damiano so that Clare could trace the sign of the cross upon him. Clare obeyed. The friar remained at the monastery a little while longer and fell asleep. On awakening, he departed, completely restored to health. Another time Francis directed to Clare ladies desirous of embracing her life of poverty and prayer. However, he did not forget to impose his will on Clare when it seemed necessary, as we have already seen when he mitigated her fasts and penances, and insisted that she accept the burden of abbess.

It was in a little cell made of reeds near San Damiano that, in the spring of 1225, after a night of torment, St.

Francis composed the «Praises of the Lord» for his creatures, known as «The Canticle of the Creatures.» Shortly afterward he also dictated «some holy words with a melody for the greater consolation of the Poor Ladies of the monastery of San Damiano, especially since he knew that they were very grieved at his illness. Since he could not visit or comfort them personally because of his illness, he wanted those words passed on to them by his companions,» (*Legend of Perugia* 45).

> Listen, little poor ones called by the Lord,
>> who have come together from many parts
>>> and provinces.
>
> Live always in truth,
>> that you may die in obedience.
>
> Do not look at the life without,
>> for that of the Spirit is better.
>
> I beg you through great love,
>> to use with discretion
>> the alms which the Lord gives you.
>
> Those who are weighed down by sickness
>> and the others who are wearied because of them,
>> all of you: bear it in peace.
>
> For you will sell this fatigue at a very high price
>> and each one [of you] will be crowned queen
>> in heaven with the Virgin Mary*.

---

* Translator's note: In October, 1976, Father Giovanni Boccali, O.F.M., discovered this text at the Poor Clare Monastery in Verona in a codex which can be dated to the first half of the fourteenth century. There is a musical setting for the English words by Father Joseph Roff.)

A few days before his death he wrote his *Last Will* for them, and Clare was careful to record it word for word in Chapter VI of her *Rule*:

«I, little Brother Francis, will to follow the life and poverty of our most high Lord Jesus Christ and of His most holy Mother, and to persevere in them till the end. And I entreat you, my ladies, and give you this counsel: that you live always in this most holy life and poverty. And guard yourselves carefully that you do not ever depart from it in any way on the teaching or advice of anyone.»

In her turn, Clare had a profound understanding of the unity in grace which bound her and her monastery to Francis. She did not think of herself as the foundress of a new Order. For her, there was one founder, Francis. She wrote in her *Testament*: «The Lord gave us our blessed Father Francis as our founder, planter and helper in the service of Christ....» The Poor Sisters are none other than «a little flock whom God the Father brought forth in his holy Church by the preaching and example of the blessed Father Francis, in following the poverty and humility of his own beloved Son and of his glorious Virgin Mother....» And as the Second Franciscan Order sprouted and grew in God's soil, thanks to Francis, so it had in Francis «our pillar and after God our solitary consolation and strength,» (*Testament of St. Clare*).

Beside him Clare considered herself nothing but «a little plant,» a shoot which Francis had planted, maintained and caused to grow. In her humility she ardently reconfirmed this at the beginning of the Rule: «Clare, unworthy handmaid of Christ and little plant of the most blessed Father Francis....» She was «the first little plant of Francis,» and also of his companions, those first «knights of the round table» who had waited in the night with lamps burning in the woods of the Porziuncula, so that she would be consecrated in that same chapel and before that same altar of the Virgin Mary, which was the center and hub of the Friars Minor. The choice of the place, the Porziuncula, was assuredly not accidental, but accorded with the desire to underscore the fundamental communion and unity of inspiration and of the form of life of the two Orders sprung from Francis, which is «to observe the Holy Gospel of our Lord Jesus Christ.»

In this light, in the light of a «little plant» which owed everything, life itself, to him who planted and nourished it in the heavenly soil, the obedience promised to Francis by Clare and in the name of her sisters (confirmed and reconfirmed many times by Clare in her Rule and Testament) went far beyond the juridical limit of recognizing the superior of the Order and became a profound relationship of dependence in the Spirit. In a manner completely to her own in the Spirit of the Lord, she shared in Francis' grace by way of obedience. Guided by him, she re-lived the same experience of faith and of love, the same experience of God, through the poverty and humility of Christ Jesus unto the beatitude of the reign of heaven which is given to the poor even in this world.

Therefore, the relationship between Francis and Clare had no need of many encounters, but was constructed on the profound dimension of faith and harmony of ideal which clothed it in a charming, spontaneous simplicity and open confidence. A page in *The Mirror of Perfection* gives proof of this in the unfolding of Francis' last days when the approach of «Sister Death» painted all things in their true colors:

«During the week in which blessed Francis died, Lady Clare, the first flower of the Poor Sisters of San Damiano in Assisi, feared that she might die before him, for they were both seriously ill at that time. She wept bitterly and could not be comforted, because she thought that she would be unable to see blessed Francis, her only Father after God, before her death, for he had been her comforter and teacher, and had first established her in the grace of God.

«So she sent word of her fears by one of the friars, and when he heard of it, the saint was moved with compassion for her, for he loved her with an especial and paternal affection. But realizing that he could not fulfil her desire to see him, he wrote a letter to comfort her and all the Sister, and sent her his blessing. And he absolved her from any fault that she might have committed against his counsel and against the commands and teachings of the Son of God. And so that she might put aside all sadness, he was guided by the Holy Spirit to say to the friar whom she had sent, "Go and tell the Lady Clare to put aside all sorrow and grief, for she cannot see me now. But promise her that before her death both she and her Sisters shall certainly see me, and be greatly comforted because of me."

«Soon afterwards, when blessed Francis had passed away in the night, all the people and clergy of Assisi came very early to take his holy body from the place where he had died, and they all sang hymns and praises and carried branches of trees. And by the will of God they bore him to San Damiano, so that the words that God had spoken through blessed Francis to comfort his daughters should be fulfilled.

«And when the iron grille through which the Sisters used to receive Communion and hear the word of God had been removed, the friars lifted the holy body from its bier and raised it in their arms in front of the window for a long while. And Lady Clare and her Sisters were comforted by this, although they were filled with grief and wept aloud when they saw themselves deprived of the consolation and counsel of so great a Father,» (*Mirror of Perfection* 108).

Francis died October 4, 1226. Two years earlier Clare had contracted the infirmity which would accompany her for twenty-nine years, until her death – twenty-nine years of love in suffering. But what was the secret of a life so pure in faith, so unswerving in its consistency, so joyous when every human joy has failed?

Chapter Four

THE PRAYER OF SAINT CLARE

The secret of Clare is her prayer, her continual standing in the presence of God. The night of her flight to the Porziuncola at the age of eighteen, she turned her back on the world, but only to turn her face to the threshold of the mystery of God. In this mystery, Clare enclosed herself, and of this mystery the material enclosure is only a sign, something which the senses perceive. Clare enclosed herself in San Damiano like a long night of prayer and of contemplation, a «night of Francis with God» protracted to a lifetime.

Between the four walls of San Damiano Clare, lost in God, rediscovered the rustling of the woods tossed by «Brother Wind,» the solitude of the grottos, the calm of Trasimeno, all imbued with colloquy of Francis, «most lowly worm» with his «most sweet God.» Clare's enclosure was the freedom which Francis enjoyed only when face to face with God, as her poverty was the empty space which the word of God excavated in her heart in order to gather there the fullness of the Good.

«Make a capaciousness of yourself, and I shall make myself a torrent,» the Lord said to Blessed Angela of Foligno. To be made poor is to possess the Kingdom, the fullness of love, communion of the Father with the Son in the Spirit. When one makes of himself a large vessel for the Spirit of the Lord, the Lord will dwell in him. To become poor ones in the full sense is to become contemplatives, to be open to the Spirit of the Lord who is the Father of the poor and who incarnated the Word in Mary.

The life of St. Clare was one single prayer. Entering the monastery at eighteen years of age, ceding her will to St. Francis and ridding herself of all things, even the right to the minimum necessary to sustain human nature, she reduced herself to that spiritual nakedness which has faith as its sole support and the glory of God as its sole wealth.

Seeking only the glory of God in every action, in prayer as in work, clinging to his will, which is salvation, Clare became the "orante," the praying one, a woman open in simplicity to union with God, to the germination of his word in the custody of her heart; a silent presence at the fountain of the mystery of God, a woman pure and strong whose hands and heart were wide open to receive, as a free and empty vessel, the torrent of grace and salvation which, in the Spirit, flows from the Father through the Son to all humanity. Clare stood poor and silent with Christ in his night on the mountain (*Lk* 6:12), in the presence of the Father, «for the life of the world» (*Jn* 6:51). For her poverty was the indispensable condition of freedom from every bond that could hinder her praise of God because «wherever your treasure is, there will your heart be too» (*Mt* 6:21), and «treasure» is everything one feels to be his own, although all things are God's.

Obedience served to strip her of herself and to give her at all times a will free of any obligation which might have impeded her full availability to God moment by moment. A truly obedient person, as delineated by St. Francis and well represented by St. Clare, is the only being on earth who is really free, because he is the only one who awaits nothing from the next moment, but reposes in the peace of the present moment and lives it solely to honor the Lord.

The enclosure springs from the summit of poverty and obedience. It is a deepening in oneself of the despoliation of Christ, «an emptying for God alone,» (*Perfectae Caritatis* 7). For Clare, the enclosure was to have the experience of the mystery of Christ who, alone on the mountain, threw himself wide open to the Father for the sake of all humanity; it was also to have the experience of the solitude of the cross, a solitude which placed her as it did Christ between the world and the Father in mediation for humanity, to bear within herself the human drama as something suffered and offered.

On the other hand, one who is stripped of all things, as well as of oneself in order to live solely through God, of God and with God, loses the taste for purely human things and feels a distaste for a life which pursues many interests and is occupied with many concerns outside of loving God and adoring him. Nothing should disturb the colloquy between Creator and creature when it pleases him to come to her, just as he came down at eventide to talk with Adam.

Life of Union with God

From the moment in which Clare consecrated all to God, she lived for nothing but God. Her living, we should say her very breathing, was but a constant contact with the object of her love, a silent and continuous colloquy with the Most High. Her face shone from the joy of this intimate living with God. She showed no trace of anxiety, and her serenity and happiness were such that they were communicated to her daughters when they merely looked at her.

She prayed much, and for Clare praying signified loving and adoring God with all her being, with all the strength he had given her. For her praying was a total return to God of her very self to the most intimate fiber of her being, purified in continual mortification, stripped in absolute poverty and in perfect obedience. She was tireless in prayer, prostrate on the ground day and night. She was never sated with contemplating and adoring her God, and from each of those prolonged intervals with him she drew a new impetus to love him and to give herself to him. She returned from prayer transformed. The sisters noticed that her visage seemed more luminous and more beautiful and that she could speak only of God. All of the Process of Canonization is a witness in this regard:

– «When she came from her prayer, she admonished and comforted her sisters always speaking the words of God who was always in her mouth, so much so that she did not want to speak or hear of vanities. When she returned from her prayer, the sisters rejoiced as though she had come from heaven,» (Pacifica di Guelfuccio, *Process* I).

– «She was assiduous in prayer. Her manner of life and speech was always concerned with the things of God so she never gave her tongue or ears to worldy things,» (Filippa di Leonardo, *Process* III).

– «She was assiduous in prayer and contemplation. When she returned from prayer, har face appeared clearer and more beautiful than the sun. Her prayers sent forth an indescribable sweetness so her life seemed totally heavenly,» (Amata di Martino, *Process* IV).

– «She was vigilant in prayer and sublime contemplation. At times, when she returned from prayer, her face appeared clearer than usual and a certain sweetness came from her mouth,» (Cecilia di Gualtieri, *Process* VI).

After Compline while her daughters slept on their hard pallets, she remained alone in prayer. Often prostrate on the ground her face was bathed in tears which the excesses of grace caused to flow copiously. Often Satan tempted her during prayer. One night while praying thus with many tears he accosted her and said, «Don't cry so much or you will become blind.» Immediately Clare replied, «No one who sees God will become blind.» The same night after matins the tempter approached her again. «Don't cry so much,» he repeated, «unless you want your brain to dissolve and flow out through your nostrils, for that would leave you with a disfigured nose.» To which Clare responded, «No one suffers disfigurement who serves the Lord,» and Satan departed.

Clare's Christ-centeredness

St. Francis used to say, that we are «the brides, the brothers and the mothers of our Lord Jesus Christ.... We are his brothers when we do the will of his Father who is in heaven, and we are mothers to him when we enthrone him in our hearts and souls by love with a pure and sincere conscience, and give him birth by doing good. This, too, should be an example to others,» (St. Francis' *Letter to All the Faithful*).

Clare was a daughter, sister and mother of Christ. She was all these in the love of Christ which consumed her. She contemplated him when, wrapped in poor swaddling clothes, his Mother laid him in the crib. She submerged herself in the mystery of the Incarnation and suffered with him while he agonized in the Garden of Olives and was thirsting on the cross. Clare lived only with him and through him. Christ was the center of her life and Clare was the vine branch which at every moment drank new sap from the vine.

The Babe of Bethlehem

The nativity always filled her with wonder and inundated her with tenderness. «Look at the border of this mirror (Christ), that is, the poverty of Him who was placed in a manager and wrapped in swaddling clothes. O marvelous humility! O astonishing poverty! The King of angels, the Lord of heaven and earth, is laid in a manger!» The saint wrote this in her fourth letter to Saint Agnes of Bohemia. In the Rule which she left for her sisters she wrote, «For love of the most holy and most beloved Child wrapped in such poor little swaddling clothes and laid in a manger, and of his most holy Mother, I admonish, pray and exhort my Sisters that they be always clothed in the garments of the lowly.»

In the Process of Canonization of St. Clare Sister Agnes of Oportulo testified that during a sermon given by Brother Philip of Atri she saw a most beautiful child about three years of age near the saint, and throughout the sermon he played with the holy virgin. The sight communicated a peculiar sweetness to Sister Agnes. Another time, Sister Frances of Capitaneo saw a baby of marvelous beauty in the lap of the saint, and she pressed him close to her while two firey wings above her head opened and closed over her, hiding her face.

Another episode merits mention. It was Christmas Eve 1252, the last Christmas Clare passed on earth. She was sick, lying down upstairs in the dormitory. Her daughters had gone down to church to recite matins before midnight Mass. She was alone. The echo of footsteps ceased. Below the nuns were exultant in the joy of the liturgy announcing the birth of the awaited one. Clare upstairs, completely alone in the dormitory, longed to be with them to celebrate the Infant wrapped in poor swaddling bands who, for love of the Father, was made flesh in the womb of the Virgin. The silence of the night did not carry even an echo to the cold, empty dormitory. «You are born, O Lord; and You have left me here alone,» breathed Clare. Alone. The night was filled with peace. Soon in Bethlehem a Babe would cry feebly in a manger. Clare thought of the Infant of Love who would be born. She felt as though he were about to come. The air seemed more pure. There was no sound to be heard. Such peace! In a moment a wail would rise from the cradle. «Lord, I am here alone,» Clare thought. «O You who are about to come, afire with love, sunlight...,» and gradually the thoughts of the saint yielded to love.

Behold! A song reached her from the distant church of St. Francis. The friars were chanting the psalms, and the organ accompanied them. The air was filled with the sounds of a choir and light. He is born! In the manger there was a baby swathed in light. The Virgin was enveloped in her ample mantle, the purest of the pure. He is born! O Babe, shining love, love, love... Such choirs, Lord, such light this night! He is born!

After the Mass, when the nuns came to their mother in the dormitory, their eyes filled with the joy of the holy night, Clare gathered them together saying, «Blessed be the Lord Jesus Christ who did not abandon me even if you did! Through the grace of Christ, I really heard all of the ceremony celebrated this night at the church of St. Francis, and I have seen the Lord's crib.»

Crucified Love

If her love of the Infant rendered her worthy to assist at his birth in joyous ecstasy, her love of the Crucified made her worthy to share in the sufferings of Christ. Her mind was as though rooted in Jesus Crucified and each remembrance of the Passion of the Lord wrung tears from her. Often she recited the Office of the Passion composed by St. Francis and taught to her by him. As a constant reminder of the sufferings of Christ, she girded herself beneath her habit with a knotted rope in addition to the cilice she usually wore. The first thing she taught the novices was to hold always in their hearts a remembrance of the Crucified, and her most stirring words were those in which she pondered again the sufferings of the Lord.

«Then, in the depth of this same mirror,» continued the aforementioned passage in the fourth letter to Saint Agnes of Bohemia, «contemplate the ineffable charity that led Him to suffer on the wood of the Cross and to die there the most shameful kind of death. Therefore, that Mirror, suspended on the wood of the Cross, urged those who passed by to consider, saying: "All you who pass by the way, look and see if there is any suffering like my suffering!" Let us respond with one voice, with one spirit, to Him crying and grieving who said: *"Remembering this over and over leaves my soul downcast within me!"* From this moment, then, O Queen of our heavenly King, let yourself be inflamed more strongly with the fervor of charity.» And truly the soul of Clare was consumed with pondering the Passion of Christ. As his Passion was approaching, Clare's suffering approached too.

On Holy Thursday the hours passed by gradually, and as afternoon yielded to evening, from the depths of her soul the anguish which Christ felt in himself in Gethsemani welled up in Clare, «sorrow unto death.» She closed herself in her cell in order to accompany with her prayer the prayer of the Lord in the garden. Absorbed in his sorrow, her soul again travelled step by step the path of her Savior, from his bloody sweat beyond the Kedron to the mocking laughter in the courtyard of the praetorium. Such was the anguish which assaulted her that her spirit fainted and, exhausted by the suffering of her whole being, identified with Christ, she let herself fall painfully onto the bed.

It was thus that she was found by Sister Filippa who, worried by the long silence, kept returning to her mother's cell. All day Friday, outside herself, Clare remained stretched out upon the bed united with her suffering Lord.

At nightfall of Saturday Sister Filippa finally returned with a candle and reminded her mother of her promised obedience to St. Francis not to go a day without taking some nourishment. At the reminder of obedience the saint returned to herself and said, «What need is there of a candle? Is it not daytime?»

«Mother, a night has passed, and another day has passed, and a second night has begun,» the daughter replied.

«Blessed be this sleep, dearest daughter,» said Clare, «since I have so long desired it. But be on guard never to refer to this (sleep) to anyone as long as I am alive!»

St. Francis taught, «Blessed the religious who treasures up for heaven the favours God has given him and does not want to show them off for what he can get out of them. God himself will reveal his works to whomsoever he pleases. Blessed the religious who keeps God's marvellous doings to himself,» (*Admonitions* XXVIII and XXII).

Clare and the Eucharist

Such were the effects of Clare's meditating again and again on the birth and passion of Christ. But if the re-living of the life of the Lord in union with him meant letting herself be totally replaced by Christ – «I live no longer I, but Christ lives in me» (*Gal* 2:20) – union with the sacramental Jesus overwhelmed her every time with reverence and trembling. Sister Benvenuta testified at the Process of Canonization that «the Lady Clare frequently received the holy sacrament of the Body of our Lord Jesus Christ, trembling all over as she did so.» (*Process* II).

The Saracens at San Damiano

There is an episode which gives very good witness to the faith and confidence of the virgin of Assisi with regard to the most blessed Eucharist. It was a Friday of

September 1240, and Saracen and Tartar troops of Frederick II's army had been dispatched around the countryside surrounding Assisi. St. Clare was upstairs in the dormitory lying on her poor bed gravely ill. Her daughters, frightened by the roving bands of soldiers, and, worse than soldiers, bandits at the very threshold of the monastery, ran to their mother seeking protection and help from her. The saint comforted them: «My sisters and daughters, do not be afraid because, if the Lord is with us, the enemy cannot harm us. Have confidence in our Lord Jesus Christ because He will free us. I want to be your hostage so that they do not do anything bad. If they come, place me before them,» (*Process* III).

Suddenly, at about the hour of none, the nuns enclosed in San Damiano heard an uproar and shrieks within the cloister walls and were terrified. Some of the soldiers had broken into the monastery by climbing over the walls and were angrily beating against the refectory door. The daughters ran to their mother and she, supported by two of them, Sister Francesca of Capitaneo and Sister Illuminata of Pisa, had herself brought down to the refectory door and there between herself and the door placed the little silver and ivory box which contained the Blessed Sacrament. And weeping she prostrated on the floor and prayed.

The two who were supporting her heard her say, «Lord, look upon these servants of yours, because I cannot protect them.» And lo! from the case containing the sacred species came the sweet timbre of a child's voice saying, «I will always defend you.» Nor did Clare forget her Assisi. «Lord, please defend the city as well.» And the same voice answered, «The city will endure many dangers, but it will be defended,» (*Process* IX). It was a dialogue of few words, but when it was over there was a great silence outside. The Saracens had withdrawn without causing damage.

The Contemplation of St. Clare

From ancient times Magdalen, seated at the Lord's feet listening to his word, has been employed as a symbol of contemplation in contrast to Martha who was too anxious about things destined to come to nothing. To Martha, disturbed because her sister was not helping her to serve, Christ replied, «Yet few (things) are needed, indeed only one. It is Mary who has chosen the better part, and it is not to be taken from her,» (*Lk* 10:42). Only the better part, love, which is never satiated with contemplating, is destined to remain in eternity.

St. Clare was called to this better part, the contemplative experience, which made of her life, of her hours of prayer as of her hours of work, of her hours of joy as of her hours of suffering, a continual contemplative search for God, a humble, hidden, assiduous experience of love. Contemplation let her gradually penetrate in depth the unfathomable mystery of God in whom is conjoined silence and words, solitude and communion, separation and presence. It was an experience of the circular movement of the trinitarian love, but even more, in the footsteps of St. Francis, of love incarnate, of the Word made flesh, laid to rest by his mother in a manger, dying naked and poor on the cross for us.

In the emptying and poverty of a fabric woven of self-same days constructed on the Gospel, Clare's life became «an attentiveness on the Lord, an adhering, an intimacy, a love, a consent, a reciprocal presence, a marveling and an admiration before the works of God, an assimilation of the Word, a solitude with him, a silence, a communion, a sharing: fulfilling God's design, salvation in the acts in which the design is realized in the Christian and, through him, in the Church,» (J. Leclercq, *Vita Religiosa e Vita Contemplativa*, Assisi 1972, 86).

Contemplation is a limitless opening to the Spirit of the Lord for the sake of the Church and the world; an offering to God of an open channel, free of everything human in poverty of being, of things, of self, in order to adhere completely to him, spirit and heart, to celebrate in him, and with him, in the Father. This is how St. Francis taught St. Clare to restore man, the «house of God going to ruin,» not in doing but in being, in making a place for God and his plan of salvation for all mankind, in becoming poverty which diffuses itself humbly and contemplatively to the Infinite. Her life of contemplation echoed Francis' cry: «Who are You, my most sweet God, and who am I, most lowly worm, Your useless servant?»

A flash of lightning rends the night of faith and kindles a light which burns quietly and brightly in the soul that is poor and at peace. The Son of God comes and makes his dwelling in the faithful soul as in the womb of Mary. «[He who is] the Truth has said,» wrote Clare, «Whoever loves me will be loved by my Father, and I too shall love him, and We shall come to him and make our dwelling place with him,» (*Letter* III).

Every conversation of the saint slipped into contemplation. It suffices to review her writings (the four *Letters to Saint Agnes of Prague*, the *Rule* for the Poor Sisters, and the *Testament*) to understand how her heart and her thought were always turned to Christ in a gaze of love. In the second letter she wrote, «Your Spouse, though more beautiful than the children of men, became, for your salvation, the lowest of men, was despised, struck, scourged untold times throughout his entire body, and then died amid the suffering of the Cross. O most noble Queen, *gaze upon Him, consider Him, contemplate Him,* as you desire to imitate Him. If you suffer with Him, you will reign with Him. If you weep with Him, you shall rejoice with Him. If you die with Him on the cross of tribulation, you shall possess heavenly mansions in the splendor of the saints,» (*Letter* II).

Clare did not write much, but like Francis all that she wrote was the fruit of her experience, of her standing with God, of her brideship in the Holy Spirit, enveloped like Mary in a veil of silence. Sister Death alone was to lift the veil slightly as she approached, revealing Clare to be «daughter and handmaid of the Most High Father,» as Francis had desired, in a marvelous spiritual childhood. «"Go calmly in peace, [my blessed soul,] for you will have a good escort, because He who created you has sent you the Holy Spirit and has always guarded you as a mother does her child who loves her.... O Lord, may You who have created me, be blessed." She said many things about the Trinity, so softly the sisters were not able to understand her well,» (*Process* III).

«This is Clare: a rainbow of prayer, a word of love, always living in the presence of the Most High, a "thank-you", joyous and childlike, which blossoms among the smallest essentials of life and resounds loudly in the Heaven of the Father, and it has a name: contemplation,» (Giulio Mancini, O.F.M., *Contemporaneità di S. Chiara*, Assisi 1954, 40).

As everything offered Clare occasion to meditate on

the love which urged God to become man, so, in the footsteps of St. Francis, for her too all creation had but one voice, and that the praise of the Lord. Sister Angeluccia remembered that when the saint sent the extern sisters outside the monastery «she reminded them to praise God when they saw beautiful trees, flowers and bushes; and, likewise, always to praise Him for and in all things when they saw all peoples and creatures,» (*Process* XIV).

For Clare the cloister was, therefore, far from being a means to flee creatures. Rather, it was the only indispensable means by which the silent word ascending from the cloister attained to God without passing through any intermediary and reached him in purity, untainted by human interests, to praise him and to speak to him of men. In the cloister St. Clare gathered into God all creatures beyond the walls of San Damiano. Much more, she gathered the whole universe into God. Detached from things, she saw them in that purest of mirrors which is God, and thus understood the true purpose of their creation, which is to give glory to God, whether trees which bow their leafy heights at the breath of the wind, or men who people the farthest limits of the earth.

«Nowhere was the strict rule of silence greater,» wrote the ancient biographer of the saint in regard to San Damiano (*The Legend of St. Clare*). Prayer which is raised in silence is consequently prayer fabricated of silence within the four walls of the cloister. But the enclosure walls were far from restricting prayer, as the saint found inspiration for praising God in all the trees, flowers and bushes,» in all men and in all the creatures that the extern sisters found on the streets of the world. Precisely because she was enclosed, because she was a woman separated from the world in the mystery of God, not for herself, but for the salvation of the world, Clare was closer to mankind. Perhaps no one is closer to man than those who, like her, live a life of prayer in a cloister where the anxieties of all men, the distress of the afflicted, and the pain of the suffering are always present and shared in the agony of Christ.

Clare said to her daughters, «I consider you co-workers of God Himself and a support of the weak members of His ineffable Body,» (*Letter* III). A cloistered contemplative knows what it means to bear the world within her in the heart of Christ as a mother bears within her the child to whom she is giving life. Thus the pure contemplative prayer of Clare often became intercessory prayer for the suffering: for little Mattiolo of Spoleto, or for the child of Sir Giovanni, the procurator of the monastery, for the sick nuns, for the lady from Pisa as well as for all of Assisi.

The Blossoming of Prodigies

Mattiolo, a three- or four-year-old of Spoleto, had poked a pebble into his nose. It was so deeply imbedded that it could not be removed in any way and the child was in danger of suffocating. In great anguish he was taken to St. Clare who traced the sign of the cross over him. Immediately the stone fell out spontaneously.

Sir Giovanni of Assisi's little boy was endangered by a disease of the lymph glands which caused a very high fever. His father, who was the procurator of the monastery, brought the little five-year-old to the abbess. After praying and making the sign of the cross, Clare sent him back completely cured.

Another child was brought to San Damiano from Perugia. One eye was completely covered by a blemish. Clare touched him and made the sign of the cross over him. Then she ordered that he be taken to her mother Ortulana who, after the death of Favarone had followed her daughter and was clothed in the habit of St. Francis. She, too, made the sign of the cross over the little Perugian boy and his eye became clear and normal.

A woman from Pisa who had been possessed by the devil returned to the monastery parlor free of every trace of possession to thank the saint for her prayer.

But Clare did not intercede before God only for children, for her sisters, for the lady from Pisa. As we saw in the Saracen assault against the monastery, Clare also prayed that the city of Assisi not suffer any harm.

The Liberation of Assisi

There is another episode which revealed the power of St. Clare's prayer before the throne of God. In 1241, the year following the Saracen assault on San Damiano, the regular troops of Frederick II's army, commanded by Vitalis de Aversa, laid siege to Assisi and summoned the defenders to surrender. After prolonged resistance the city was about to fall. When this was reported to Clare, she assembled the nuns. The episode was narrated by Sister Francesca di Capitaneo, who was one of them.

«Lady Clare called her sisters and said to them: "We have received many benefits from the city and I know we should pray that God will protect it." She therefore said they should come in the morning for some time with her. When they had come, the Lady made them bring her some ashes. She took all the coverings from her head and made all the sisters do the same. Then, taking the ashes, she placed a large amount on her newly tonsured head; after this she placed them on the heads of the sisters. Next, she directed all of them to go pray in the chapel. So it happened; being broken and defeated, the army left the following morning. From then the city of Assisi did not have another army over it. And on that day the sisters abstained and fasted on bread and water; some of them did not eat anything on that day,» (*Process* IX).

Clare responded to the charity which fed her with the charity of prayer. To the generous Assisians who supported San Damiano the saint responded with the prayer which liberated the city from siege.

Clare's Opening to the World

Contemplative prayer, which was Clare's way, opened her to the world, and consequently her prayers were intercessory. It is precisely here in prayer that the cloister of San Damiano opened to establish a relationship between the saint and mankind. In God Clare had an immediate comprehension of all human problems; in God she was more than ever close to man and to all creatures. But in their turn men and creatures brought her back to God, because they spoke to her of him who is Creator, Redeemer, God-made-man for love of men. The prayer of St. Clare was a current of love flowing from God to men and returning again to God from men. The enclosure was the only means through which this movement could be fulfilled. What is the purpose of this, someone might ask. We can answer with a page from Romano Guardini:

«It can be compared with our Lord seated at Bethany and Mary bringing precious nard to Him, pouring it on His sacred feet, drying them with her hair, and the fragrance filling the whole house. A niggardly soul murmured: "Why so much waste?" But the Son of God admonished: "Let her do it; it is for the day of my burial." There was a mystery there of death, of love, of fragrance and of offering. So too with incense: it is a mystery of the beauty which ignores all reason, but rises freely; of love which burns ardently, is consumed and dies. Here too the barren spirit presents itself and asks: "To what purpose is all this?"

«The same passage says that the prayer of the saints is an offering of perfume. Incense is a symbol of prayer, and of that prayer which has no seeming purpose; which desires nothing and which ascends like the Gloria after every psalm; which adores and longs to thank God "because He is so great and magnificent...." But there can also be a superficial emotion of love of God that comes from shallowness of feelings, from a barrenness of heart, like the murmuring of Judas Iscariot.

«In such a person, prayer is reduced to a sort of spiritual merchandise, and in that sense, it is certain to be measured by worldly standards. However, this mentality is unacquainted with the regal plenitude of the prayer that wants only to give. It is entirely ignorant of profound adoration, and of that soul of prayer which demands no "why" nor "to what purpose," but ascends because it is love and fragrance and beauty. And the more it loves, the greater is the offering and the perfume which rises from the fire which has consumed it.» (R. Guardini, *I Santi Segni*, Brescia 1954, 81-84).

CHAPTER FIVE

THE «HIGHEST POVERTY»

In the years following the death of St. Francis (1226), Clare seemed to be engaged above all in maintaining his ideal of poverty. The community of Poor Sisters in Assisi continued to increase. Beatrice, Clare's youngest sister, was among others who entered San Damiano in 1229. At about the same time, following Favarone's death, her mother Ortolana entered.

However, the Order was spreading beyond Assisi and even outside Italy. In 1234 on the feast of Pentecost Saint Agnes of Bohemia, daughter of King Ottokar, entered the monastery of Poor Clares in Prague. Only four of the letters which St. Clare wrote to Agnes have come down to us. These represent a valuable source of information concerning the spirituality of the saint of Assisi and as such we have made frequent reference to them. «The kingdom of heaven is promised and given by the Lord only to the poor for she who loves temporal things loses the fruit of love...,» Clare wrote in the first of these letters. Elsewhere in the same letter she wrote, «O blessed poverty, who bestows eternal riches on those who love and embrace her! O holy poverty, God promises the kingdom of heaven and, in fact, offers eternal glory and a blessed life to those who possess and desire you! O God-centered poverty, whom the Lord Jesus Christ who ruled and now rules heaven and earth, who spoke and thinks were made, condescended to embrace before all else!

«The foxes have dens, He says, and the birds of the air have nests, but the Son of Man, Christ, has nowhere to lay his head, but bowing his head gave up his spirit.

«If so great and good a Lord, then, on coming into the Virgin's womb, chose to appear despised, needy, and poor in this world, so that people who were in utter poverty, want and absolute need of heavenly nourishment might become rich in Him by possessing the kingdom of heaven, be very joyful and glad! Be filled with a remarkable happiness and a spiritual joy! Because, since contempt of the world has pleased you more than its honors, poverty more than earthly riches, and you have sought to store up greater treasures in heaven rather than on earth, where rust does not consume nor moth destroy nor thieves break in and steal, your reward is very rich in heaven! And you have truly merited to be called a sister, spouse and mother of the Son of the Most High Father and of the glorious Virgin,» (*Letter* I).

Imitation of the Poor Christ

This is one of many passages of St. Clare's writings in which she exhorts to poverty. Here one notes the immediacy of her passing from exhortation to contemplation, to which we alluded in the preceding chapter. She is transported instantaneously from poverty in the abstract to the contemplation of the poor Christ. For her poverty makes sense, and full sense, not so much as a means to mystical exaltation (and far less as an end to be achieved), but as an expression of love of the poor Christ.

Since he had no place to lay his head, Clare too would

be so poor as to have no place to lay her head. Because he had no dwelling place or property or even a garment, since even this was torn from him before the crucifixion, neither would Clare have a house or goods or garment, and that which necessity imposed she would possess only in the way in which Christ possessed, that is, granted to her moment by moment by the bounty of the Father.

Before God Clare was «the poor one» par excellence. By the will of the most high heavenly Father, under the guidance of Francis, she spent her life in a material and spiritual poverty that was severe, hard, bare and total, and which Clare herself had to call by many names in her Rule in order to be understood: «poverty, labor, trial, scorn and contempt of the world,» (*Rule of St. Clare* VI).

This initial experience of her religious life, as though proposed by Francis to test her Gospel vocation, but also continuous for the whole course of her life, emptied her of every possible security outside of God, denuded her of every possible illusion, of every attachment and of every expectation that was not an expectation of God alone, of him, the Lord. It was a presence which inebriated with joy the humble and poor heart thrown open to him in a prayer of love «in the secret of the Father,» (*Mt* 6:6).

«Happy, indeed, is she to whom it is given to share in this sacred banquet so that she might cling with all her heart to Him..., whose kindness fulfills, whose affection excites, whose contemplation refreshes, whose kindness fulfills, whose delight replenishes, whose remembrance delightfully shines,» (*Letter* IV).

The kingdom belongs to the poor. The plenitude of goodness asks only an emptiness into which he can be gathered. Clare's poverty was a radical poverty, capable of carving out this empty space even in the most intimate depths of her heart. It was a kenosis, a vast gamut of poverty, obedience, love of humiliation, able to fall on its knees before the most high Father, not only in body but in that depth of the human being where the «I» of pride is nested.

One does not become humble, poor by oneself without first enjoying and rejoicing like Clare in this inheritance of «poverty, labor, scorn and contempt of the world,» which was the inheritance of the Son of God and of his poor little Mother, and which ever will be their way. «Let her [most high poverty] who leads you into the land of the living be your portion,» (*Rule of St. Clare* VIII). Francis said, «A person is really poor in spirit when he hates himself and loves those who strike him in the face,» (*Admonitions* XIV).

Clare was well-instructed on the significance of poverty by the Poverello who wrote in his Testament: «Those who embraced this life *gave everything* they had to the poor. They were satisfied with one habit which was patched inside and outside, and a cord, and trousers. *We refused to have anything more;*» and also, «The friars must be very careful not to accept churches or poor dwellings for themselves, or anything else built for them, unless they are in harmony with the poverty which we have promised in the Rule; and they should occupy these places only as strangers and pilgrims,» (*Testament of St. Francis*). In the first Rule for his Friars Minor he wrote, «The friars should be delighted to follow the lowliness and poverty of our Lord Jesus Christ, remembering that of the whole world we must own nothing; but having food and sufficient clothing, with these let us be content, as St. Paul says,» (*Rule* IX).

In his following of the poor crucified Christ Francis' measurement was the measurement of lovers. The same was true of Clare, a lover like Francis. By example he taught his «little plant» that man has need of nothing if it be not the will of God, and man must seek nothing but the kingdom of God which belongs to the poor.

«Think of the ravens,» the Gospel says, «they do not sow or reap; they have no storehouses and no barns; yet God feeds them. And how much more you are worth than the birds! Think how the flowers grow; they never have to spin or weave; yet, I assure you, not even Solomon in all his royal robes was clothed like one of them. Now if that is how God clothes a flower which is growing wild today and is thrown into the furnace tomorrow, how much more will he look after you, who have so little faith! But you must not set your hearts on things to eat and things to drink, nor must you worry. Your Father well knows you need them. No; set your hearts on his kingdom, and these other things will be given you as well,» (*Lk* 12:24 ff.).

This was exactly Clare's poverty as reflected in the sources: *naked faith*, a throwing open of herself before the Father with limitless faith in the Gospel promises given to the poor, an abandoning of herself without reckoning to the «Father of Mercies,» who is «the giver of every good thing» and before whom «we ought to ponder the immense favors of God bestowed on us,» (*Testament of St. Clare*). Hers was an attitude of utter freedom with a heart liberated from every human preoccupation, free «as the sparrows of the sky» in the hand of that Father, the Most High, who knows the number of our hairs and who knows what his children need, (*Lk* 12:22-32).

Beyond the walls of San Damiano Francis begged from door to door, having made himself poor for the love of Christ, content all his life with a coarse tunic and a cord. Inside the same walls Clare defended herself until her death against anyone who desired to separate her from the «most high poverty» which made her «sister, mother and spouse of Christ.»

The Privilege of Poverty

As soon as she entered San Damiano, she had her share of her patrimony distributed among the poor. «She kept nothing of its worth for herself, and gave it all to the poor. Thus, after leaving the world outside and enriching her mind within, she ran after Christ without being burdened with anything,» (*The Legend of St. Clare*).

In the year 1215 or 1216 she besought the Holy See for the so-called «Privilege of Poverty,» a unique document of its kind, in which the Pope sanctioned the saint's desire that no one might constrain her or her followers to accept possessions.

«Since you have sold all things and given them to the poor,» Gregory IX wrote in 1228 in the second redaction of this document, which is the very foundation of Clare's Gospel experience, «you propose not to have any possessions whatsoever, clinging in all things to the footprints of Him, the Way, the Truth, and the Life who, for our sake, was made poor. Nor does a lack of possessions frighten you from a proposal of this sort; for the left hand of the heavenly Spouse is under your head to support the weakness of your body.... Finally, He who feeds the birds of the heavens and clothes the lilies of the field will not fail you either food or clothing....»

For Clare, the heavenly Father was that Father of whom she could say at life's ending that «He has always guarded you as a mother does her child who loves her,» (*Process of Canonization* III); and she could bless him and thank him before Sister Death as «a poor lady» who received gratuitously from him. «May You be blessed, O Lord, You who have created my soul!»

Clare always respectfully opposed and firmly refused the same Pope Gregory IX who further exhorted her to accept property which could provide income for the monastery. And, though he assured her, «If you fear for your vow, We absolve you from it,» the saint replied, «I will never in any way wish to be absolved from the following of Christ.» (*Legend of St. Clare*).

In her Rule (1253) traced along the lines of the First Rule of St. Francis and the Regula Bullata of 1223, she prescribed, «If, by divine inspiration, anyone should come to us desiring to embrace this life..., let the words of the holy Gospel be addressed to her: that she should go and sell all that she has and take care to distribute the proceeds to the poor,» (*Rule of St. Clare* II) «for the love of that Lord who, laid poor in a manger, lived poor in the world, and remained stripped on the cross,» (*Testament of St. Clare*).

The Rule's sixth chapter, which sprang entirely from her heart, is rich in autobiographical and Franciscan memories. In it she reaffirmed the concept she expressed more and more frequently to her sisters, «that their dwelling-place would be acceptable to God only when it was rich in poverty, and that it would continue to be secure by the strong watchover of the most exalted poverty,» (*The Legend of St. Clare*).

The entire Rule of St. Clare, in fact, speaks of poverty continually, from the beginning which states the Order is to be called «the Order of the *Poor Sisters*» to the particular details of the common life: «for the love of the most holy and most beloved Child wrapped in such poor little swaddling clothes and laid in a manger, and of his most holy Mother, I direct, pray and exhort my Sisters that they be always clothed in the garments of the lowly,» (*Rule of St. Clare* II). She underlines holy poverty again in the evangelical and ecclesial closing: «always submissive and subject at the feet of that holy Church, unwavering in the Catholic faith, we may forever observe the poverty and humility of our Lord Jesus Christ and his most holy Mother and the holy Gospel which we have firmly promised,» (*Rule of St. Clare* XII).

It was not only in words that the saint maintained her life of poverty. When the brothers returned from their begging, it was not the unbroken loaves which rejoiced her, but the scraps that people had offered in charity. She received these with special joy as being more in keeping with that state chosen first by Francis and embraced by her in imitation of him.

Never did the voice of the saint resound with such warmth as when she exhorted to poverty, and never did her words find so many obstacles in those who heard them. It assuredly is not easy to understand this tenacious love for an absolute poverty which feels every least possession as well as every material preoccupation with tomorrow (unless it be within the order willed by God) to be an insupportable weight for one whose life has but one goal, the glory of God himself.

Poverty does not necessarily mean begging. He who holds out his hand to a fellow man with avidity to possess is far less poor than he who has many possessions without being attached to his goods. There are poor persons who hate unto death those who might deprive them of the little they have; there is the man who has but a single possession and is capable of killing anyone who might take it from him. These are not the poor, even if they are ordinarily judged to be so by the world. It is not these of whom Jesus said, «How blessed are the poor...: the kingdom of heaven is theirs,» (*Mt* 5:3). *The poor,* rather, are those who are indifferent as to whether they have or have not; they are all those on the face of the earth who are happy with whatever the Lord gives them, being convinced that it is precisely enough to render to God the maximum praise which he asks of them. *The poor* are those who are serene in the will of God manifested moment by moment, and they use what they have to fulfill that will without deviating, without losing themselves in daydreams or building in vain, but in the present reality using all that God puts at their disposal to glorify him, moment by moment.

It is also true, however, that it is written, «If you wish to be perfect, go and sell your possessions and give the money to the poor, and you will have treasure in heaven; then come, follow me... And everyone who has left houses, brothers, sisters, father, mother, children or land for the sake of my name will receive a hundred-times as much, and also inherit eternal life,» (*Mt* 19:21,29).

The Necessity of Poverty for the Contemplative Soul

«If you wish to be perfect...,» says Jesus. It is an invitation. But to one who loves him, such an invitation becomes a command, and so the Master further exhorts, «Be perfect as your heavenly Father is perfect,» (*Mt* 5:48). Although strictly speaking, he is poor who, even though possessing much is not attached to his goods, for the man who intends a stricter following of Christ, every possession feels like an intolerable weight. Any property becomes a stumbling block, a bondage which prevents the soul from freely following the Lord where he wishes to lead it. This, in fact, is the greatest fruit of poverty, a freeing of the soul from everything in order to render it available for God's full possession.

One could say that as one gradually despoils himself completely (stripped of things by poverty, stripped of self by that supreme form of poverty which is obedience) the grace of God finds more space to expand and to act, and the more the grace is extended, the more the soul feels as a burden every possession that is not God alone. Therefore, absolute poverty is at the same time a need of the soul thirsting for God alone and a manifestation of the work which grace has accomplished and continues gradually to perfect the soul. He who loves God with his whole heart, his whole mind and all his strength, and aspires, as does every lover, to be united with his beloved, cannot desire anything but God and feels encumbered by whatever might retard the race to him.

Thus it was for Clare. Deprived of every natural and human support, she became free, empty, open, available before the plenitude of good which gushes forth like a fountain of joy from the bosom of the Father of mercy and overflows filling the hearts of friends with «hidden sweetness,» (*Letter* III). Even the remembrance of this plenitude of the good makes the heart beat quickly: «...Whose rememberance delightfully shines,» (*Letter* IV) and invites, urges, presses one to be ever more poor, more empty, poor by the standard of Francis, and to be, like him, a capacity for God, «the All Good.»

For a long time the bare earth was her bed, a stone from the river her pillow, and the smallest morsels of bread her food. A monastery in poor repair was her shelter for the forty-two years of her monastic life. In the bare rooms of San Damiano Clare experienced what it means to be poor, cold, hungry, fatigued from work, and to consider all this to be supreme wealth. It is not possible to understand the choice of such a life except, as we have said, as the threshold opening wide into a life of grace which superabundantly compensates for the sacrifice of all possessions.

Nor did it suffice for the saint to lack all things for herself. She wanted to guarantee juridically that her sisters would be incapable of any form of possession. Benvenuta of Perugia testified: «She especially had a greater love of poverty. Neither Pope Gregory nor the Bishop of Ostia could ever make her consent to receive any possessions,» (*Process of Canonization* II). These words were echoed by Pacifica di Guelfuccio and Filippa di Leonardo (*Process of Canonization* I; III).

It was the security for tomorrow which St. Clare battled against with all her strength. And yet, it would seem that a minimum fixed income would assure bread as well as order and regularity in the life of prayer in a community of sisters. However, it is also true that possessions would be a limitation put on providence, which promises the hundredfold in this life in addition to eternal glory to whomever leaves all. To provide for tomorrow, in the final analysis, is to put more trust in human means than in God, to decline the hand of God extended to us, overflowing with every good, in order to prefer the hard, stale bread and piece of fruit withered with age. It is a question of faith.

He who does not believe feels the need to provide for himself; he who believes God's promises does not accumulate things nor does he feel a need to make provision for tomorrow.

For Clare, security was the word of God, and she accepted no other guarantee. Hers was a poverty which made persons *itinerants* in a journey of faith, from Exodus toward the Promised Land, without human security, without an established dwelling in this world, without a place to rest one's head, like Christ, because, Clare repeated with Francis, «the foxes have their dens, and the birds of air have nests, but the Son of Man has nowhere to lay his head,» (*Letter* I). Clare lived enclosed in the narrow ambit of four cloister walls, an itinerant in faith and in poverty. It was the journey of one who traveled toward the kingdom and never arrived, nor ever would arrive here below, but who experienced at every instant the haste of the paschal night.

«The pact that she had established with holy poverty was so great and brought such love, that she wanted to have nothing but Christ the Lord and would not permit her sisters to possess anything,» (*The Legend of St. Clare*). In fact, in the Rule she wrote, «The Sisters shall not claim anything as their own, neither a house nor a place nor anything whatsoever; and as pilgrims and strangers in this world, serving the Lord in poverty and humility, let them confidently send for alms... since the Lord made himself poor in this world for us,» (*Rule of St. Clare* VIII).

Not even her beautiful San Damiano, the monastery rebuilt by Francis among the olive trees of Mt. Subasio where Clare's entire existence was consumed, not even the four walls of the most rigid enclosure had the power to deter Clare from her spiritual going forth «as a pilgrim and stranger in this world.» Like Francis, re-clothed in the poverty of the Lord Jesus and of his poor little

Mother, she did not swerve from this journey in faith and poverty which knows but one abode as its own, *the poor, crucified humanity of the Lord Jesus*.

Clinging to him, to him alone, as a poor little virgin, without encumbrance of baggage for the way, without a staff to lean on, without a change of garments, without a purse, as is written in the Gospel (*Mt* 10:10; *Lk* 9:3, 10:4), Clare became one with crucified, suffering humanity before the fullness of the one good, the Father, who fills the long night of human suffering with overflowing joy and pervades it with interior, certain light. It was the prime secret of the strong, poor, pure, single-minded and confident Clare, until her final «Go *calmy in peace*, my blessed soul,» (*Process of Canonization* III).

The Response of Providence

Providence was solicitous on its part to keep the promise and to intervene, even miraculously, when the efforts of the Poor Ladies did not suffice to provide the necessities of life. Cecilia di Gualtieri, dispenser of the monastery, recounted at the canonical process an episode which confirms what we have been saying up to now.

It was dinner time and hunger was pressing. Only one loaf of bread remained in the monastery, one loaf for fifty nuns (at that time the community had grown), and for the brothers who assisted them. Clare sent for the dispenser and ordered her to divide the loaf in two, sending half to the brothers. The other half she was to slice into fifty pieces and to distribute them to the nuns who were already at table. Cecilia, surprised by such a command, looked with amazement at her mother and said, «My mother, the Lord's miracle of the five loaves and two fishes would be needed to make fifty slices out of that!

«Go and do as I have told you,» the saint replied. Cecilia began to slice the bread and as she cut, the bread increased between her hands until fifty thick slices had accumulated in the basket (*Process of Canonization* VI). On that day too the bread of providence did not lack on the table of the Damianites.

The bread... but the love of God knows subtleties which men rarely achieve. Upstairs in the infirmary an extern sister lay gravely ill. As a good mother, the saint herself cared for her. For some time the patient had refused all nourishment. Lovingly the saint asked, «Sister, is there something you could eat or would eat with pleasure?» The sister who had lost all appetite due to the gravity of her illness and believing that those foods could not be obtained given the distances between Topino, Nocera and Assisi, responded, «Yes, I would willingly eat trout from the Valley of Topino and a cake from Nocera.»

However, the charity of the saint was not such as to be stopped by requests so disarming. Clare prayed to God on her knees to provide for the needs of her sick daughter. Little by little evening descended and with the falling shades a pouring rain also began. In the darkness and in the midst of the heavy shower someone rapped insistently on the monastery door. Surely it was one of the brothers. But the sister who ran to open the door found a young man who, without a word, held out a napkin knotted by the four corners. She ran to take it to the holy mother so that after removing the contents, the napkin could be returned to the youth waiting outside. Behold! the trout and the cakes requested by the invalid. The young man, invited to remain with the friars because of the late hour and bad weather, refused and departed rapidly. There was nothing for the saint to do but to thank the Omnipotent who once again had provided for the needs of the Poor Ladies.

Saint Clare and Work

It would be erroneous to think that the poverty embraced in so radical a manner by St. Clare and her daughters was a rash resorting to the help of neighbors. On the contrary, St. Clare exhorted her daughters to work with alacrity, and the generosity of others was called upon only when the work did not suffice for life's needs.

It was thus that they were taught by their Saint Francis who wrote in his *Testament*, «And I work with my hands and I want to work and I desire that all the other brothers work at labor that is honest. Those who do not know how to work should learn, not because of a desire to earn a recompense from their work, but to give good example and to avoid laziness.» He permitted recourse «to the table of the Lord,» that is, to alms, only «if there should be no payment for his labors,» (*Testament*).

Nevertheless, work should always be of a kind that fosters the spirit of prayer and never suffocates it. Because if the union of the soul with God is impeded, the work would fail the very purpose of poverty, which is to free the soul, rendering it more available to the action of grace. For this reason Clare wanted her daughters «to so work with their hands during certain hours that, according to the desire of the Founder, they would keep warm through the exercise of prayer and, fleeing the lukewarmness of neglect, would put aside the coldness of a lack of devotion by the fire of holy love,» (*The Legend of St. Clare*).

In Chapter VII of the Rule she prescribed that «The Sisters to whom the Lord has given the grace of working should labor faithfully and devotedly after the hour of Terce at work which contributes to integrity and the common good; and this in such a way that idleness, the enemy of the soul, being banished, they do not extinguish the spirit of holy prayer and dedication whose purpose all other temporal things ought to serve.»

Clare carefully followed a hierarchy of values. Work was to be seen in relation to prayer as a help to it rather than placed beside it in importance. Nor was work to have as its sole or principal good the procuring of support for the sisters. Rather, for St. Clare work was a requirement of love which, continually rekindled in prayer, could not but overflow into action as St. Catherine says in her *Brief Dialogue on Consummate Perfection*. «As the little vessel placed beneath the fountain overflows when it is full and irrigates the earth which surrounds it, the little receptacle of the soul, beneath the fountain of God's love, when it is full, turns the beneficent waters inward on itself without ever becoming empty.»

For St. Clare the prime purpose of work was to love God in action just as he is loved in contemplation. In fact, it can be said that for St. Clare there was no longer a difference between prayer and work, because both arose from contemplative love and had one end, which was more contemplative love. For this it no longer mattered whether or not work had a relatively commensurate recompense. To St. Clare it was important that the labor testified to love of God and supported prayer, not that the remuneration would be such as to provide for the needs of the community. Just as her prayer was prayer for the purpose of the praise of God, so her labor was labor for the coming of the reign of God.

St. Francis prescribed that the friars were to work wherever they happened to be without ever requesting recompense, but that they were to be content with whatever was given them. Even this was not to be considered as reimbursement for their labor, but as alms bestowed by the charity of their fellow man. This was so, too, for St. Clare, «the little plant,» who was concerned that her daughters work, but not to earn a living, and that after having worked, they should stand very simply like the truly poor with hands outstretched humbly for the charity of others. Divine providence which clothes the lilies and feeds the ravens would provide even more for his children.

St. Clare's Corporals

Here, too, St. Clare was mistress more in deed than in word. Although infirm, she did not, therefore, cease working, but «never wanting to be idle at any time, made herself rise, sit up in bed and spin,» Sister Cecilia di Gualtieri testified (*Process of Canonization* VI). She arranged to have the pillow propped up and thus spun fine linen with which she made corporals – fifty pairs of them, counted by Sister Francesca di Capitaneo. She placed them in small silk cases and entrusted them to the brothers to be distributed to poor churches scattered about the surrounding mountains and valleys. Thus, when St. Clare's lips ceased praying, her hands began: and lips and hands testified to the overflowing of the little vessel under the flood of God's love.

CHAPTER SIX

«GO IN PEACE, MY BLESSED SOUL!»

Even the last years in the life of the saint, to say nothing of the final months, were occupied with the defense
of absolute poverty. In 1251 the illness which Clare had
contracted in the distant year of 1224 became aggravated
to the point that her imminent homegoing to the Lord
was feared.

«Virtue is brougt to perfection in sickness.... (And) her
marvelous virtue... (was) perfected in her sickness...: because during the twenty-eight years of her prolonged
sickness "she did not murmut or utter a complaint" but
holy comments and thanks-giving always came from her
mouth,» (*The Legend of St. Clare*). On the contrary, Clare
never ceased praising God, admonishing the sisters to
perfect observance of the Order and especially the love
of poverty (*Process of Canonization* XIII).

With the worsening of the illness, the sisters pressed
around their mother more than ever, anxious lest from
one moment to the next she be without their affection.
But God made it clear that the saint would live until the
papal curia, which that year happened to be at Lyons,
would come to Assisi.

A vision of this was granted to a Benedictine nun at
the Monastery of San Paolo, the same monastery in
which Clare had stayed at the beginning of her religious

life. It seemed to the nun that she and her sisters were at San Damiano to assist the sickly Clare and that the saint lay on a costly bed. While they were weeping, awaiting the death of the virgin, a. stately lady appeared at the head of the bed and spoke thus to the mourners: «Do not cry, daughters, for she will continue to live since she cannot die until the Lord comes with his disciples.»

Sovereign Visits

At the end of that year, the fifth of November, 1251, Pope Innocent IV arrived at Perugia with his court. On September 8, 1252, the poor «little plant» of St. Francis received a visit from Cardinal Rainaldo Segni, bishop of Ostia and Velletri, her devoted friend and protector of the Order. He gave Clare the Body of the Lord and preached a sermon to the assembled community. Taking advantage of this visit, the saint begged the Cardinal to intercede with the Pope to confirm in perpetuity her *form of life* in poverty.

Actually, the Rule approved by the Apostolic See which the Damianites were observing while Clare awaited Sister Death on the little cot in the infirmary, was not the one which she wished to leave in perpetuity as the norm of life for her present and future daughters. Clare had drawn up her own Rule, which included the little primitive rule given her by Francis, his oral and written counsels and, above all, the essence of the Privilege of Poverty.

It is this Rule which she warmly entrusted to the Cardinal of Ostia, imploring him to press the Pope for the definitive approval. On 16 September, Cardinal

Rainaldo reassured the abbess of San Damiano on this subject in a letter, «Quia vos,» which subsequently was inserted into the Bull of Innocent IV, «Solet Annuere,» of August 9, 1253.

In the course of 1252 the Pope and the Cardinals moved from Perugia to Assisi. The vision of the passing of the saint was about to be fulfilled. The disease raged with greater intensity in Clare's body, already wasted by long years of infirmity. She had an intuition that the end was nearing.

The Pope together with the Cardinals hastened to visit the poor Damianite. «Since he considered her life to be beyond that of the women of our time, he did not hesitate to honor her death with the papal presence,» (*Legend of St. Clare*).

He entered the monastery, was directed to her pallet and placed his hand near the face of the invalid so she could kiss it. In a transport, she asked also to kiss his foot. The Vicar of Christ mounted a wooden bench and presented his foot, on which the saint reverently laid her face and kissed the instep and sole. Then she asked for the remission of her sins, and her face was illumined with joy in anticipation of the sacrament she was about to receive. The pontiff exclaimed, «Would to God that I had no more need of pardon than she!» He imparted a general absolution and the apostolic benediction. Brother Angelo, the minister provincial of the Friars Minor, gave her the Body of Christ.

When Clare was again alone with her sisters in the silence of San Damiano, tears of compassion bathed her face, and she said to her daughters, «Praise the Lord, my children, because today Christ has condescended to give me such a blessing that heaven and earth are not enough to compensate for it. Today... I have received the Most High and have been worthy to see his Vicar!» (*The Legend of St. Clare*).

A Long and Serene Agony

But the Lord was coming closer and stood almost at the threshold. The saint began her long agony. For seventeen days she ate nothing. Little by little as material strength abandoned her, it was replaced by a spiritual strength which even permitted her to comfort all those who came to visit her. The enclosure doors opened to the many Cardinals who came to her day by day to draw strength as though from a saint. She exhorted all to a more perfect service of God.

In the fields outside, August was triumphing. In the infirmary of San Damiano Clare asked the brothers to remain close to her and to keep recounting the passion of the Lord. Those present included Brother Leo, the friend, companion, confessor and advisor of St. Francis. Weeping, he kissed the bed of the dying saint. Present also was Brother Angelo, one of St. Francis' first companions who, though weeping himself tried to console the nuns. «When Brother Juniper appeared among them, that excellent jester of the Lord...,» St. Clare «was filled with a new joy and asked him if he had anything new from the Lord. When he opened his mouth, he burst forth with words that were like burning sparks coming from the furnace of his fervent heart. The virgin of the Lord took great comfort in his parables,» (*The Legend of St. Clare*).

The night between Friday and Saturday, August 8 and 9, 1253, the sisters who were keeping vigil with the dying

Clare heard her speaking after a long silence. «Go calmly in peace, for you will have a good escort, because He who created you has sent you the Holy Spirit and has always guarded you as a mother does her child who loves her.... O Lord, may You who have created me, be blessed,» (*Process of Canonization* III). And then she added many things about the most blessed Trinity, but with such subtlety that the nuns could not follow her.

«To whom is Mother speaking?» the astonished daughters asked. One of them approached her and asked, «Mother, to whom are you speaking?»

«I am speaking to my blessed soul,» the saint replied.

The hour of death was an hour of joy. As the dying Francis wanted his brothers around him repeating his «Canticle of the Creatures,» so Clare blessed the Lord for having created her soul and lovingly guiding her as a most tender mother loves her dearest child. Nothing could obtain greater joy than the security of having spent every breath of one's life for the glory of God. All the sisters, fearful and weeping, were gathered around Clare. «O daughter, did you see the King of Glory whom I saw?» the saint repeatedly asked those closest to her (*Process of Canonization* IV).

A Multitude of Holy Virgins Visits St. Clare

Sister Benvenuta turned her glance toward the door. Behold, a multitude of virgins in white garments with gold crowns circling their heads! «Among these virgins,» Benvenuta related, «there was one greater, above and beyond what could be described, far more beautiful than all the others, and wearing a crown upon her head larger than all the others. Above her crown she had a golden cluster in the form of a thurible from which such a brilliance came forth it seemed to illuminate the entire house.

«These virgins approached the bed of the holy Lady Clare. That virgin who seemed greater at first covered her bed with the most delicate cloth so fine that, even though she was covered with it, Lady Clare nonetheless saw through its great delicacy. Then the Virgin of virgins... inclined her face above the virgin Saint Clare.... After this was done, they all disappeared,» (*Process of Canonization* XI).

All day Saturday Clare was in agony. Sister Filippa testified that she seemed to cling to life only because of her desire to see confirmed by papal Bull the Rule which assured the most rigorous poverty to the nuns that were present and to come. In fact, Sister Filippa heard her express her deep desire to have the Rule of the Order approved by the Pope so that she might kiss the seal of the Bull and then die immediately (*Process of Canonization* III).

The Confirmation of the Rule

And that is actually what happened, because on August 10, one of the friars brought the longed-for papal confirmation in the Bull «Solet Annuere», given in Assisi August 9, 1253, and containing the Rule which the saint had desired for herself and her daughters for all time. Clare received it with emotion and devotion and, despite her weakness, lifted it to her lips to kiss it.

«On the following day, Lady Clare, truly clear without

stain, with no darkness of sin, passed from this life to the Lord, to the clarity of eternal light,» concluded the testimony of Sister Filippa (*Process of Canonization* III).

On Monday evening August 11, 1253, the feast day when Assisians commemorated and still commemorate their patron St. Rufino, Clare died happy to begin to live in him who always «had guarded her like a mother the little child whom she loves.»

Conclusion

Perhaps it would be useful to dwell here on the many miracles worked by St. Clare after her death and which hastened the initiation of the canonical process (November 1253) that led two years later to her canonization by Pope Alexander IV (1255). But we proposed only to delineate the figure of St. Clare of Assisi who is close to us through her sanctity, and sanctity does not consist in miracles, which are only a proof of holiness, not its substance. Sanctity is adhering to the will of God, whatever it might be, fully and generously, instant by instant, whether that will call one to a life of prayer and penance in a cloister as it did St. Clare, or whether it summons one to a life of action on the byways of the world.

What is essential is not to invert the value scale which puts the glory of God in the first place and our egoism in the last place and then, as a consequence, places us at the disposition of God and his plan for universal salvation, without sparing of strength and without limitation of any kind. «Only one thing is necessary...,» as is written in the Gospel, to love God. All the rest, when one loves God with all one's heart, with all one's mind, with all one's strength, comes about by itself, as God himself has promised. This is the great lesson which comes to us from the Poor Lady, Clare of Assisi, to whom Francis taught the secret of that joy which «no one shall take from you,» (*Jn* 16:23).

BIBLIOGRAPHY

ARMSTRONG REGIS J., *Clare of Assisi. Early Documents*.
Preface by Mother Veronica Namoyo, New York/
Mahwah, Paulist Press, 1988.

ARMSTRONG REGIS J., *Clare of Assisi. The Mirror Mystic*,
in *The Cord* 35 (July-August 1985), 195-202.

ASSELDONK OPTATUS van, *The Holy Spirit in the Writings
and Life of St. Clare*, in *Greyfriars Review* I (1978),
93-104.

BARTOLI MARCO, *Clare of Assisi*, translated by Sister
Frances Teresa, Quincy, Illinois, Franciscan Press,
1993.

BOCCALI GIOVANNI, *Textus opusculorum S. Francisci et
S. Clarae*, S. Mariae Angelorum-Assisii, 1976, 167-218.

DE ROBECK NESTA, *St. Clare of Assisi*, Milwaukee, Bruce
Publishers, 1951; reprinted, Chicago, Franciscan Herald Press, 1981.

Clare Centenary Series. An Eight-Volume Series in Honor
of the Birth of Saint Clare, General Editor HONE
MARY FRANCIS. *Towards the Discovery of Clare of Assisi:
Clare: Formed by Francis* (vol. I); *Clare Discovers the
Love of God in the Church* (vol. II); *Clare's Form of
Gospel Life* (vol. III); *Fraternal Life* (vol. IV); *Commun-
ion with Christ in the Writings of the Clares* (vol. V); *A
Compendium of Resources for a Study of St. Clare* (vol.
VI); *Clare of Assisi: Investigations* (vol. VII). Te Be

112

Announced, Vol. VIII. New York, The Franciscan Institute, St. Bonaventure University, 1992-1993.

IRIARTE LAZARO, *The Order of Poor Clares*, in *Franciscan History: The Three Orders of St. Francis of Assisi*, trans. Patricia Ross. Chicago, Franciscan Herald Press, 1979.

LAINATI CHIARA AUGUSTA, *The Enclosure of St. Clare and the First Poor Clares in Canonical Legislation and Practice*, in *The Cord* 28 (1978), 4-15, 47-60.

O'BRIEN CELSUS, *The Story of the Poor Clares,* Limerick, Ireland, Franciscan Friary, 1992.

OMAECHEVARRIA IGNACIO, *Escritos de Santa Clara y Documentos contemporaneos*, 2a ed. Madrid, Biblioteca de Autores Cristianos, 1982.